ZEN POEMS OF CHINA AND JAPAN

THE CRANE'S BILL

ANCHOR·PRESS
·DOUBLEDAY·

By Lucien Stryk

WORLD OF THE BUDDHA
HEARTLAND: Poets of the Midwest

Poetry

Taproot
The Trespasser
Notes for a Guidebook
The Pit and Other Poems
Awakening

Edited and Translated by Lucien Stryk and Takashi Ikemoto

ZEN: Poems, Prayers, Sermons, Anecdotes, Interviews
AFTERIMAGES: Zen Poems of Shinkichi Takahashi

By Takashi Ikemoto

ZEN: Weg zur Erleuchtung

ZEN POEMS
OF
CHINA AND JAPAN

THE CRANE'S BILL

TRANSLATED BY LUCIEN STRYK AND TAKASHI IKEMOTO
WITH THE ASSISTANCE OF TAIGAN TAKAYAMA, ZEN MASTER

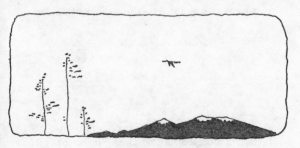

Anchor Books
Anchor Press/Doubleday
Garden City, New York
1973

ANCHOR BOOKS EDITION: 1973

895.6
5928z

DRAWINGS BY RAYMOND DAVIDSON

ISBN: 0-385-04624-3
Library of Congress Catalog Card Number 73–75168
Copyright © 1973 by Lucien Stryk, Takashi Ikemoto
and Taigan Takayama
All Rights Reserved
Printed in the United States of America
First Edition

The translators are honored to dedicate this volume to
Zenkei Shibayama Roshi,
Abbot of Nanzenji Temple, Kyoto

Thanks are due to the following periodicals in whose pages some of these poems have appeared: *12 Death Poems of the Chinese Zen Masters, Stinktree, American Poetry Review, Chicago Review, Literature East & West, New: American and Canadian Poetry, New Statesman, Seizure,* and *Transpacific.*

CONTENTS

LUCIEN STRYK's most recent of five books of verse are *The Pit and Other Poems* and *Awakening*. His poems and essays have appeared in anthologies and periodicals, and he has received prizes for his verse and a grant, along with Takashi Ikemoto, from the National Translation Center to translate Zen poetry. He is editor of *World of the Buddha*, the anthology *Heartland: Poets of the Midwest*, and translator (with Ikemoto) of *Zen: Poems, Prayers, Sermons, Anecdotes, Interviews* and of *Afterimages: Zen Poems of Shinkichi Takahashi*. He has given poetry readings throughout the United States and England, has twice been a visiting lecturer in Japan, and presently teaches at Northern Illinois University.

TAKASHI IKEMOTO, educated in English literature at Kyushu University, is Emeritus Professor of Yamaguchi University and currently teaching English literature at Otemongakuin University in Ibaraki City. He is a Zen follower of long standing with a firsthand knowledge of Christianity, and a co-translator into Japanese of a volume of Thomas Merton's essays on Zen and Enomiya-Lassalle's *Zen: Weg zur Erleuchtung*. His major concern for years has been the introduction of Japanese Zen to the West, and he has collaborated with Lucien Stryk on many Zen articles, on *Zen: Poems, Prayers, Sermons, Anecdotes, Interviews* and *Afterimages: Zen Poems of Shinkichi Takahashi*.

TAIGAN TAKAYAMA, Zen master, was recently named a successor to Zenki Shibayama Roshi, Abbot of Nanzenji, Kyoto, one of the most important Zen temples in Japan. He graduated in History of Chinese Philosophy from Kyoto University in 1951, at which time he began his studies at Nanzenji. In 1958, he was appointed chief priest of Toshunji Temple in Yamaguchi. Director of the Council of Social Welfare of his city, and of the prefectural Association for the Protection of Cultural Properties, he is also Director of the Yamaguchi Orphanage, which is subsidized by the prefecture and is located on the grounds of Toshunji.

FOREWORD

"Alas, seeing, I saw him not; meeting, I met him not. Now I repent and bemoan it as much as I did then." This sentence is found in a monumental inscription Butei (464–549), Emperor of Ryo, compiled in memory of Bodaidaruma (Bodhidharma in Sanskrit), the first Zen Patriarch in China. Butei was called Emperor Buddhamind, so faithfully did he devote himself to the Buddhist's good works. In his days Buddhists vied with one another in translating and annotating Indian sutras, building temples, carving or casting Buddhist images or providing for bonzes (monks); and he was the foremost Buddhist of the day. It was around 520 that Daruma arrived in China from India. Butei, receiving him in audience, told him that he had accumulated a great number of merits. To which Daruma replied, "No merit." Daruma's bit of repartee was apparently intended to be a radical criticism of the Buddhism of that time, a type of Buddhism engrossed in trivialities, ignoring the prime essential to the Buddhist, i.e., awakening to the Real Self. What the Patriarch wanted to convey was not that there was no need of supporting Buddhist communities, etc., but rather that to be engrossed in trifles in ignorance of the essential was meaningless and of no avail. As long as one did not lose sight of the essence of Buddhism, one would be able to behave with real profit like the then Buddhist followers. However, Butei failed to grasp Daruma's intent; and the latter left him and settled down in Shorin Temple beyond the Yangtze River. When Butei heard of the Patriarch's death, which occurred many years later, he, with great repentance, erected the monument mentioned above. This then is what happened to the intelligent emperor, and one is reminded of how unaccountable are the encounters of life.

This book is a joint effort of the three of us. Years ago, through Professor Takashi Ikemoto's introduction, I had a talk with Lucien Stryk in my temple, which eventually led to the publication of this volume. Our encounter was not of such fundamental significance as that of Daruma and Butei, and yet I deeply feel the mystery of karma in life.

In this Foreword I would like to discuss briefly how Zen and Zen poetry are related to one another. First, let me consider the essentials of Zen. The most important thing in Zen is, as Daruma pointed out, to awaken to the Real Self. It is to become conscious of the Formless Self; it means going beyond not only spatial or material forms, but psychic or conceptual forms as well, that is, truth/falsehood, beauty/ugliness, good/evil, etc. This Zen type of Self-consciousness cannot be treated as an object as in psychology or metaphysics. Ordinary self-consciousness, which can be treated in that way, is a differentiated and limited one, having a form. The Self-consciousness of Zen is what can in no way be objectified or differentiated, because it invariably remains the subject instead of becoming an object. In Zen, awakening to the Real Self is termed seeing into one's nature (*kensho* in Japanese). An ancient master restated it as "seeing *is* nature."

Thus the Zennist's Self-consciousness is totally devoid of form. Rinzai (Chinese, ?–867) states: "Mind is formless, permeating the whole universe." The *Diamond Sutra* gives a warning: "Whoever wants to see me through form or to seek me through sound is on the wrong track and will never meet the Tathagata [i.e., Buddha]." In the Soto sect, frequent reference is made to the dictum "Body and mind have fallen off." All this points to the Formless Self. Here the reader may have the mistaken notion that the Formless Self can be understood conceptually. But Zen detests conceptualization. In one of his mondos (questions and answers) Rinzai uses the expression "a real man of no titles." He says: "In the naked flesh-mass exists a real man of no titles. He is always coming in and out through your sense-organs. If you don't know him yet, look! look!" A monk, stepping forward, asks, "Who is the real man of no titles?" Rinzai climbs down from his chair and, gripping him, demands, "Speak! speak!" The poor monk hesitates, whereupon the master lets go of him, reviling, "What, he's no better than a lavatory spatula, this real man of no titles!" and hastens back to his room. In his every word and motion is revealed the master's refreshingly vivacious and firm stand on Zen activity and Zen principles.

At this point, a brief explanation of the method of Zen discipline will not be out of place, since it will help in the appreciation of Zen poetry, especially the poetry of satori (awakening). Zen, ever since its inception, has had for its motto the statement: "Pointing directly to one's mind/ Let one see into one's nature to attain Buddhahood." This is to say that Zen cannot be taught through the medium of letters and doctrine, but that it must be experienced immediately and by one's own efforts. The Real Self or the Original Self is above learning or receiving from others. Ganto (Chinese, 828–887) once said: "What enters through the gate is not one's family treasure." Any Zen master, therefore, sees to it that each of his disciples be rigorously trained to get enlightened for himself without being taught. To that end, the master may give his disciple a koan (Zen question) such as Joshu's "What is Nothingness?" or Hakuin's "What is the sound of one hand clapping?" But he never teaches him (even if the disciple cannot grasp the point of the koan, say, for ten years); the master only testifies to his disciple's understanding.

Here is a typical story of self-discipline in Zen. Kyogen (Chinese, ninth century) first studied Zen under Hyakujo, but, handicapped by his "sagacity," he could not comprehend Zen till his master died. Then he went for guidance to Isan, an enlightened senior monk. Isan said to Kyogen, "I'm told that studying under our late teacher Hyakujo, you used to give ten pat answers to one question. But, you see, that was your sagacity, discrimination based on discursive thinking; it's the very cause of the delusion of life and death. Now, tell me in a word who you were before you were born." Nonplused by Isan's challenge, Kyogen, back in his room, examined all he had ever learned, and yet he was incapable of finding even a single word to present to Isan. He said to himself that a picture of rice cake could keep off no hunger. More than once he begged Isan to expound for him, only to be rebuffed by the latter with: "If I tell you, you'll be sure to censure me one of these days. What I expound is my own satori; it's nothing to do with your satori." At last, despairing of success, Kyogen burned up all his notes on Zen and left Isan to spend the rest of his days as a common bonze. He went and stayed at the site where National Teacher Echu of Nanyo had resided when alive, looking after Echu's grave. (One should note that the greater was Kyogen's resignation, the deeper was his unconscious absorption in his problem.) One day, cleaning the garden with his broom, he chanced to send a stone flying against a bamboo close by. At the clinking sound, he had a thorough awakening. He hurried back to his hermitage, where, after purifying himself, he burned incense toward where Isan lived and thanked him, saying, "You're more kindhearted than my parents. If you'd taught me at that time, how could I have gained the blissful satori I've had today?" Then he composed the following poem of satori:

> One strike—all knowledge gone.
> No more dabbling.
> The old path discovered, I stride,
> Traceless, anywhere.
> Who knows me now?
> Dare any not approve?

Isan, when informed of the poem, approved of it with this remark, "Kyogen has penetrated." Kyogen's brother-monk, Gyozan, however, refused to admit that it was penetrating enough, and both of them subjected themselves to harder discipline till they became great masters. When satori came to him, Kyogen composed a poem; but how one expresses oneself at the moment of this Zen experience depends on the situation, the enlightened person's previous career, etc. One student may make a bow, another may thrust out his fist; while one master may approve with "You have penetrated," another with "Who knows whether my true Zen will be trampled to death by a blind donkey?" All this goes to confirm that, in spite of different attitudes held by the disciple and the master, the former has gained an insight into the Formless Self, while the latter testifies to it.

What, then, is Zen poetry? There is a form of poetry used for preaching in Indian Buddhist scriptures. In Zen literature, too, there is found a group of poems apparently descended from this traditional type: for example, *The Song of the Way* (*Shodoka* in Japanese), *The Song of Faith and Mind* (*Shinjinmei*) or *The Jewel-Mirror Samadhi* (*Hokyo Zammai*).* Further, there is a large body of poetry, completely independent of the scriptural tradition and peculiar to Zen literature; it is metrical commentary on koans, found in koan collections such as *Hekiganroku, Shoyoroku, Mumonkan,* as well as in Patriarchs' writings. The poems selected for this book are those of satori, death and general subjects.

In his *Analects,* Confucius characterizes in a word the basic feature of *The Book of Songs:* "There is no evil thought in it." The Preface to the same book states: "Poetry is an expression of thought. What is in the mind is thought; expressed in words, it becomes poetry." Apart from the problem of literary or metric forms, these remarks, I think, clarify one of the fundamental characteristics of Zen poetry; and herein, despite the Zen sect's

* These poems, however, avoid the somewhat lengthy repetitive verse form in the scriptures.

xiv

negation of letters, there seems to lie the possibility of Zen experience necessarily taking the form of verse when it gives itself literary expression. In this way there has all along been a close relationship between poetry and Zen. Poems of satori and death are poetic expressions of the Formless Self at the most significant moments in life, of satori and death respectively. Poems on general subjects are likewise versifications in various situations of that void Self. I will refrain from touching further upon the characteristics of Zen poetry since they are discussed by Lucien Stryk. What I would like to emphasize is the importance of always grasping the Zen personality which vitalizes Zen poetry and makes it the most refreshing of verse.

We are now in the midst of highly advanced civilization which has no match in human history. But frequent reference is made to man's mechanization, loss of subjectivity, decay of life and liberty. People the world over hunger after leisure, to go hiking across fields and mountains, or to enjoy sports and shows. Some of them sit in religious meditation or even use drugs, all to isolate themselves from the outer world. Conscious or not, this is escapism on the part of those who have failed to confront modern civilization; in it is revealed the basic self-contradiction of modern civilization. Man seeks to achieve an endless evolution, which, however, is blocked by what he has created for himself. Man's life is decaying. To overcome such self-contradiction, to restore lost subjectivity, life itself, is an urgent problem for all mankind. Escapism of the type mentioned above is but a makeshift, not a radical solution. It is in the overcoming of the self-contradiction of modern civilization that the *raison d'être* of Zen lies. To awaken to the Formless Self and work as "a real man of no titles"—this is to restore one's free subjectivity, embodying in oneself the Zen saying, "Today the bird, come out of its old cage, flies with the clouds."

Our translation is, in a sense, a thing of no merit just as Daruma declared. Yet, if the reader, inspired by the poems in this volume, discovers his original Formless Self, then he, unlike the penitence-stricken Butei, will have done a thing of great merit for himself.

Taigan Takayama

Yamaguchi City, Japan
May 1972

INTRODUCTION

It is high time for Western intellectuals to turn more
attention than ever to the appreciation of Zen poetry.
Hitherto, on the whole, they have been indifferent to it;
and yet, both in China and Japan, Zen poetry, pro-
claimed to be the glory of Zen literature, has always been
enjoyed with great zeal by Zen adherents. True, Zen it-
self will be attained by the unlettered, too; but those
Zennists who are incapable of appreciating Zen verse
must be considered unlucky in that they are ignorant
of a highly intriguing and inspiring area of Zen writ-
ing.

The reason why Zen-conscious Westerners have not
turned with great interest to Zen poetry is not hard to
find. The fault was not theirs; it was that of the exposi-
tors of Zen to the West. No doubt, the time was not yet
ripe for them to introduce Zen poetry to the West; they
had to occupy themselves in writing about what Zen is.
Still the fact remains that those expositors, with one or
two exceptions, were not writers of English poetry, with
the result that the Zen verse they happened to render

into English was anything but poetry. Naturally such prosaic verse could not have engaged the serious attention of the Western intelligentsia. It was with this situation in view that Lucien Stryk and I began contributing English translations of Zen verse to Western periodicals and editing them in book form. The present volume is the third of the kind, and this time we have been fortunate in receiving the co-operation of Reverend Taigan Takayama, a young Zen master.

In what follows, I want to explain several points that Master Takayama's Foreword and Lucien Stryk's Preface do not deal with or have touched upon only lightly. But, first, a few words about Zen experience that bear directly on the subject of the poetry.

One of the Zen dicta is: there is no Zen where there is no satori. Satori is the most important Zen experience; it is immediate, and no amount of pondering or philosophizing in itself can produce it. To attain satori, one must take a leap not to faith as with Kierkegaard, but to the final fact: Nothingness, as revealed in "green willow and red rose" or in Dogen's "body-and-mind fallen off" or in Rinzai's "real man with no titles." This leap may be called the *Kopernikanische Wendung* in the practical phase of human life. It is no wonder that Zen has stressed the all-importance of "No dependence upon letters and words." All masters have discouraged their disciples from pious as well as secular reading, urging them to concentrate upon zazen (sitting in Zen) or koan training to gain satori. And yet the fact is that numberless Zennists have had an awakening while reading a Buddhist sutra or a Zen writing, or hearing a sutra recited or listening to words uttered in a mondo (Zen question and answer). To give one or two examples: Hakuin (1685–1768), who was blessed with far more satoris than most Zennists, had an awakening when he came across this phrase in Master Kido's writing: "It's for you the leaves stir up a breeze." Satori came to Eno, the sixth Patriarch, at the moment he heard another recite, from the *Diamond Sutra*, "Residing nowhere, let your mind arise." It is well known that a great number of Zen followers attained enlightenment during a mondo. No one can shut his eyes to the conspicuous role letters and words have played in Zen discipline.

The point is that in Zen one must fathom more than the ordinary dualistic meaning of letters and words; that is, one must intuit Nothingness or Buddhahood, identifying oneself with it. And this typical Zen experience is depicted more vigorously and succinctly in poetry than in prose. Appealing directly to one's feeling and volition, as poetry in general does, Zen poetry is more likely than Zen prose to enable one to make the leap to the ultimate Truth or, at least, deepen one's sense of Zen.

What, then, is Zen poetry? A traditional answer will be of as much help to the reader as a subjective opinion. It is traditionally held that what basically marks Zen poetry is its embodiment of Zen truth based on satori. Because "Zen truth" here is meant in a broad sense, no clear-cut distinction can always be made between Zen and secular poems. Some critics may look upon a given poem as a piece of secular verse; others may see it as an expression of the Zen spirit. The important thing in appreciation of Zen poetry is, therefore, to sharpen the discerning eye, which in turn calls for maturing of Zen experience on the part of the appreciator. No one without Zen experience—and of course the more matured the experience, the better—can hope to be an appreciator or critic of Zen poetry. Be that as it may, the following points will be of some use for the beginning reader of this particular type of verse.

First, verse *form* has nothing to do with Zen poetry, which can be in the mode of classical Chinese verse (in four lines, etc.), of Japanese waka (thirty-one syllables), haiku (seventeen syllables), free verse or indeed in any Western verse form. Most of the poems in this book are in the form of four-line Chinese verse.

Second, the use of Buddhist or Zen terms in itself does not make Zen poetry. It is not those religious terms but the presence of Zen principle or Zen "sense" that creates Zen poetry. For instance, a mere aspiration for Zen with insertion of Zen phrases will not produce Zen poetry.

Third, the Zen priest can write secular verse, and the enlightened layman can compose Zen poetry. So-called "five-temple monks" in Japan (fl. in the fourteenth century) produced a great volume of non-Zen verse; on the other hand, Sotoba (Chinese, 1036–1101) and other laymen left behind them Zen-spirited poetry.

Next, in considering Zen verse, one must take note not only of the Zen principle of satori but of Zen dynamism or activity (*zenki* in Japanese) as well; because though a poem motivated by the Zen principle is a piece of Zen verse, there can be no good Zen poetry if Zen dynamism is missing in the verse. Zen dynamism is at once the vitality of Zen and the animating kernel of Zen poetry. Daito's (1282–1337) death poem is a good example of verse that contains this dynamism:

> To slice through Buddhas, Patriarchs
> I grip my polished sword.
> One glance at my mastery,
> The void bites its tusks.

There is no need to cite non-dynamistic poems for comparison; one can easily surmise that, without its own dynamism, Zen verse will be soulless, dead. And in appreciating this particular quality of vitality, a knowledge of *kikan* and *kigo* will be found helpful.

In present-day Japan, Rinzai Zen discipline is conducted on the basis of the so-called "Hakuin's koan system." Speaking of koan in its broadest sense, any and every thing in daily life can be a koan to be solved with one's whole body and mind. Still, as is now well known, there are traditional koans, orthodox Zen questions. Zennists customarily say that there are 1700 koans in round numbers, the reason being that the *Keitoku Dentoroku,* a standard Chinese Zen biography, treats of 1701 Buddhas and Patriarchs in all. True, there are several old collections of koans, such as *Hekiganroku, Shoyoroku, Mumonkan,* all compiled in China, or *Kaiankokugo* compiled in Japan. But in these collections, koans are not arranged systematically. It was Hakuin who first made a systematic classification of koans, solely for the effective enforcement of Zen training and not necessarily for the purpose of a scientific analysis of koans.

In Hakuin's koan system,* Zen questions are divided into eight categories in order of progressive disciplinary stages:

> 1. Dharmakaya koans, which enable the student to see into Dharmakaya, i.e., Buddhahood, suchness, etc. Of koans of this type, the best known are Joshu's "Nothingness," Hakuin's "Sound of one hand clapping" and "One's original face before one's parents were born."

* For what follows I am to a degree indebted to Master Ryomin Akizuki's *Koan* (in Japanese).

2. The category of *kikan*, which will be touched upon separately later.

3. The verbal koan, which may be exemplified by utterances of Joshu, the Radiant-lipped. For example, his "You just drink a cup of tea," irrespective of the differing responses of three monks. In Rinzai Zen, the student, after he has gained satori, is trained in the fine and proper use of words, utilizing a book of Zen phrases, etc.

4. The category of "difficult" koans, which includes Master Goso's (Chinese, ?–1104) "A buffalo's horns, head and hoofs have all passed out of his enclosure, but his tail cannot. Tell me why."

5. Those advanced koans by which the trainee transcends all the four preceding groups of koans so as to remain unattached to anything in the world. For instance, there is Master Tan of Hakuun's (Chinese, 1025–72) saying: "Several Zennists came from Rozan. They've all gained insight into their Nature, know how and why, and have responded with fitting comments. Only, they're far short of the mark."

6. The Soto Zen master Tozan's (Chinese, 807–869) theory of five grades. In this theory, the five-fold relationship between the absolute and relative is probed, the last being the grade of complete unification of all opposites.

7. The ten major prohibitions, in which the ten Buddhist commandments (kill not, steal not, etc.) are re-examined. In Zen, those commandments are meant for the Formless Mind, the Zennist being trained to reach a mental state wherein he rises above commandments, neither observing nor violating them.

8. The final-barrier koan with which koan study

ends: a question devised by each individual master. For example: "Say in one word all Rinzai's utterances."

Here I must return to the second category of koans, the applied, inasmuch as it more directly concerns the essentially literary quality of Zen verse. The applied koan is called *kikan* in Japanese. *Kikan* originally meant a craftsman's skillful device, an instrument which moves of itself, a skillful means. The *kikan* is designed to train those students who have solved the Dharmakaya koan and attained satori; that is, to assist the enlightened student with applied koans in living freely amid complexities of life instead of remaining complacently in the non-differentiated state of satori. A study of *kikan* koans is so-called "discipline after satori" or "maintenance of the correct mind." The foregoing is the essential explanation of the applied koan, but a little more may be said about it.

The *kikan* is a koan of dynamism (*zenki*). It is in *kikan* koans (almost all koans are said in a sense to be *kikan* koans) that Zen dynamism is most brilliantly in evidence. Dynamism as life-activity beyond all that is relative, life/death, good/bad, rich/poor, etc. Zennists' winks, cries, blows, all an expression of Zen dynamism, are most likely to come to the fore in examination of *kikan* koans. And in koans of this type, Zen dynamism takes the form of dynamic or active word (*kigo* in Japanese) either in a narrow or a broad sense. To give a few examples of proper dynamic expressions which are apparently extremely irrational:

a. Run a horse in the bowl.

b. Today the very ice shoots flame. (No. 3 in this book.)

c. The eastern mountain moves along the stream. (Tenth-century Chinese master Unmon's answer to a monk's question "Where were Buddhas born?")

N.B. There are a good number of *kikan* feelers, such as "Bind space with a rope and bring it to me," "Blow out a light a thousand miles away," "Enter this pillar and come out."

Zen treats a seemingly ordinary saying as an expression of Zen dynamism; for example, Joshu's "Well, clean your bowl" in the following mondo:

> Monk: I've entered your monastery. Please give me instructions.
> Joshu: Have you eaten gruel?
> Monk: Yes, sir.
> Joshu: Well, clean your bowl.

What essentially distinguishes Zen poetry is the spirit of dynamism, dynamic expressions, though one may not often come across such expressions in the proper narrow sense. It is these spiritual and stylistic features that make Zen poetry inspiringly invigorating. I have briefly discussed the Zen experience of satori, so-called "No dependence upon letters and words" in relation to satori and Zen poetry, the characteristics of Zen poetry, and finally the koan system, especially *kikan, zenki, kigo*. What follows concerns more technical matters calling for the reader's attention.

As regards the poems in this volume, we have selected shorter pieces, most of which have in the originals four, or rarely six to eight, lines written in classic Chinese, the rest being Japanese wakas, etc. The reason for the stress on Chinese is simply that, under Chinese influence, even Japanese Zennists, ancient and modern, were prone to write classic Chinese verse. And, in both China and Japan, shorter pieces are customarily preferred apparently because brevity and pithiness fit into the spirit of immediate Zen experience. Furthermore, shorter Zen poems are, on the whole, less doctrinal than longer ones, a fact conducive to our purpose to present Zen verse rich in literary flavor. (One must recognize the fact, however, that the Chinese master Yoka's *Song of the Way*, a long piece of 267 lines, for example, has a depth of inspiration all but unparalleled in world religious verse. Of this poem, there is only Daisetsu Suzuki's literal English translation; a rendering in good poetic English is yet to appear.) The Chinese poets are naturally older and belong to the eighth to thirteenth centuries, while the dates of the Japanese range from the twelfth to the twentieth centuries, the older periods being more fully represented. Of some Zennists no exact dating is possible; in such cases the century, which is sometimes only approximate, is mentioned. The poems are not arranged chronologically. Rather their content has been a larger consideration in their ordering.

As for the pronunciation of the names of Chinese Zennists and places, Japanese enunciations are given. Which to choose, for brevity's sake, of the two names forming the Zennist's full name is often problematical; one might say it all depends on arbitrary custom. For instance, in the case of Chosha Keishin (No. 4 in our volume), the first name is usually cited; in that of Mugaku Sogen (No. 81), the second is normally preferred. Full names can be given, but then Dogen's full name, Kigen

Dogen, for instance, would sound strange; the single name Dogen is now so familiar to us. We have, therefore, tried to give the more familiar name if there is one, excepting the cases of the Zennists whose full names are usually mentioned. In dubious cases, which necessarily arise, we had to decide somewhat arbitrarily.

Our translation had to be free as in previous Stryk-Ikemoto renderings of Zen poetry. (See *Zen: Poems, Prayers, Sermons, Anecdotes, Interviews*, New York, Doubleday; *Afterimages: Zen Poems of Shinkichi Takahashi*, Chicago, The Swallow Press, and London, London Magazine Editions.) It follows that in four-line Chinese poems, for example, the formal line-by-line semantic structure of inception, following-up, variation, conclusion is not necessarily apparent in our translations. For again, our major objective was to bring out the Zen spirit and Zen dynamism in the form of present-day English poetry, and to this Lucien Stryk applied both his sense of Zen and his poetic abilities. Whether or not we have succeeded is for the reader to judge himself. But this must be said: our renderings are at times quite different from those of other expositors of Zen.

Our explanatory notes on the poems themselves call for explanation. Basically, Zen poems, like koans, are objects not of ordinary lectures but of Zen lectures (*teisho* in Japanese). A Zen lecture differs from an ordinary lecture in that it is more than a mere verbal elucidation of facts; its aim is to open the listener's eyes to satori, and, to this end, the Zen lecturer, i.e., Zen master, employs any means, words, silence, gestures, etc. One of the simplest forms of Zen lecture or, one might say, Zen demonstration, is that of the old Chinese master Gutei, who, in reply to any religious query, lifted one of his fingers. The following is a brief account of a Zen lecture delivered by Joko Shaku, a modern Japanese master (reported by one of his disciples):

Master Joko's *teisho* was on the Chinese poet Sotoba's satori poem:

> The mountain—Buddha's body.
> The torrent—his preaching.
> Last night, eighty-four thousand poems.
> How, how make others understand?

The master, after analyzing it, said that the most important words in the poem were "mountain" and "torrent." With growing interest, he continued, "Then, which of the two words is more important? Of course, 'torrent.' Well, then, what's the torrent? What's the sound of the torrent Sotoba heard at Rozan? I'll say 'Zaa-zaa-zaa!' The sound filling the whole universe!" After a pause: "Good. Then, is the torrent alone the Buddha's profound teaching?" After another pause, he went on, "Oh, I forgot about the mountain. What's the mountain? I'll have to let you see it." Then he turned down his lower eyelid with a finger, saying, "Do you see any green in my eye?"

Naturally, our notes are not of the *teisho* type; they are no more than a pointer to the verbal meaning of the poems. We just hope that the reader will sense or penetrate the fundamental Fact of Zen to which the poems themselves are also pointers.

Now it is my pleasure to mention the warm cooperation Master Taigan Takayama has kindly given. He provided for us the original readings of the greater part of the verse in this volume, prepared his explanatory notes, looked into the dates of birth and death of some of the poets and answered our questions about poems and notes. Without his co-operation, our book would not have been put together. It must be noted, however, that he is not responsible for the translation of the poems. For that and for most of both the interpretation of the poems and the commentary on them, Lucien Stryk and I are to be held solely responsible.

English translation of Zen verse is no easy task. As things stand now, it seems to require collaboration of English-speaking poets and Japanese Zennists. Even such collaboration will not always guarantee complete success. All we can hope is that our joint translation will meet the need for English rendering of Zen verse, so that Western people might gain a better understanding of Zen Buddhism.

Takashi Ikemoto

Nagaokakyo-shi, Kyoto-fu, Japan
October 1972

PREFACE: ZEN POETRY

One spring day in 1912 the German lyric poet Rainer Maria Rilke had an extraordinary experience, which based on the poet's account to her the Princess Marie von Thurn und Taxis-Hohenlohe described in the following manner:

> He wandered absent-minded, dreaming, through the undergrowth and maze of briars, and suddenly found himself next to a huge old olive tree which he had never noticed before. . . . The next thing he knew he was leaning back into the tree, standing on its gnarled roots, his head propped against the branches. . . . An odd sensation came over him so that he was fixed to the spot, breathless, his heart pounding. It was as though he were extended into another life, a long time before, and that everything that had ever been lived or loved or suffered here was coming to him, surrounding him, storming him, demanding to live again in him. . . . "Time" ceased to exist; there was no distinction between what once was and now had come back, and the dark, form-

less present. The entire atmosphere seemed animated, seemed unearthly to him, thrusting in on him incessantly. And yet this unknown life was close to him somehow; he had to take part in it. . . .

The princess was of course suitably impressed, and saw the experience as further proof of the poet's otherworldliness, romantic disposition. Had Rilke spoken with a Zen master of the event, it would have been called perhaps by its right name, spiritual awakening. Zen Buddhism's main purpose is to make such experiences possible, for their result is liberation.

Because Zen exists as a discipline to make an awakening possible, and because its adherents are made aware, early in their training, that all their labors will be fruitless unless they are enlightened, many have at least simulacra of the event. If in the West the mystic realization is extremely rare, in the Zen communities of the Far East it is consciously worked for, induced in a thousand and one ways. Often the Zennist writes a poem expressing the essence of his awakening, the depth of which is suggested by the quality of the poem.

Zen is unique as a religion-philosophy of artistic manifestation, the attainments of its practitioners often gauged by the works of art they make. The disciple is expected to compose poetry of a very special kind (*toki-no-ge* in Japanese, or "verse of mutual understanding") on the occasion of the momentous event which the solving of his koan, or problem for meditation, always seems to be. Koans are set disciples by the masters so as to make them realize that there are things beyond the reach of common sense and logic, that the sensible normal way of handling things does not always work and that if they hope to win enlightenment they must break through the barriers created, in all of us, by "mind." Satori poems are always genuine because only those winning the approval of the poet's spiritual guide are designated as such: the poet does not himself refer to a poem as an enlightenment poem before the fact of his master's approval.

As a consequence of the anciently established practice a rather natural process of criticism and selection takes place: what has passed down as satori poetry is in other words the cream—the rest, what in fact was not reproduced, was for some reason found wanting (this is true only of awakening poetry: "death" poems are written only by mature and established masters who have earned the right to be heard at such a time, and "general" poems written by those masters whose words are considered important enough to preserve). Enlightenment poems rejected by masters are sometimes, as the result of the poet's later eminence, reproduced, as in the case of the Chinese master Chokei, the first of whose satori poems following was rejected, the second approved:

> Rolling the bamboo blind, I
> Look out at the world—what change!
> Should someone ask what I've discovered,
> I'll smash this whisk against his mouth.

*　　*　　*

> All's harmony, yet everything is separate.
> Once confirmed, mastery is yours.
> Long I hovered on the Middle Way,
> Today the very ice shoots flame.

It would be presumptuous even to try to imagine why the first of these poems was rejected as lacking sufficient insight by Chokei's master (to assume that it was its "arrogance" would be risky, as many true satori poems seem even more "arrogant"), but the second is surely an extraordinary poem. Only the master, aware of his disciple's barriers, can determine whether a breakthrough has been made: if it has, the poem will show it. Such judgment, considering the spiritual context, places the highest sort of value on art. The most famous example in Zen history of the manner in which a satori poem is written, and the tremendous consequences it can have for the writer, is recounted in one of the most important Zen texts, the *Platform Scripture* of the Sixth Patriarch of Zen in China, Hui-neng:

> One day the Fifth Patriarch, Hung-jen, called all the disciples together and said: "Life and death are serious matters. You are engaged all day in making offerings to the Buddha, going after blessings and rewards only. You make no effort to achieve freedom, your self-nature is obscured. How can blessings save you? Go and examine yourselves—he who is enlightened, let him write a poem, which, if it reveals deep understanding, will earn him the robe and the Law and make him the Sixth Patriarch. Hurry, hurry!" Shen-hsiu, the senior monk, wrote:

> > Our body is the tree of Perfect Wisdom,
> > And our mind is a bright mirror.
> > At all times diligently wipe them,
> > So that they will be free from dust.

> Then the humble Hui-neng, who as a mere "rice pounder" was practically unknown in the monastery, wrote in response to Shen-hsiu's poem:

The tree of Perfect Wisdom is originally no tree,
Nor has the bright mirror any frame.
Buddha-nature is forever clear and pure.
Where is there any dust?

Which so impressed the Fifth Patriarch that Hui-neng was named his successor, saying: "You are now the Sixth Patriarch. The robe is the testimony of transmission from generation to generation. As to the Law, it is to be transmitted from mind to mind. Let men achieve understanding through their own effort."

Death poems are perhaps the most unusual of the Zen poems: rarely morbid, self-serving or self-sorrowful, and never euphemistic, they serve a uniquely spiritual end, as inspiration for the master's immediate followers and for the Zen community at large. The tradition of the death poem is very old, and as with many traditions it perpetuates itself. Expected to write such a poem, the master not only steels himself for the task but for death itself. He is as a Zennist expected to face the inevitable stoically, and he does not fail his disciples. There are many anecdotes about the valor, before death, of the masters, the following being well known:

When a rebel army took over a Korean town, all fled the Zen temple except the Abbot. The rebel general burst into the temple, and was incensed to find that the master refused to greet him, let alone receive him as a conqueror.

"Don't you know," shouted the general, "that you are looking at one who can run you through without batting an eye?"

"And you," said the Abbot, "are looking at one who can be run through without batting an eye!"

The general's scowl turned into a smile. He bowed low and left the temple.

In the Zen communities not only the masters were expected to write death poems. The greatest of the haiku writers Matsuo Basho (1644–94) was asked by his friends, when it was clear that he was about to die, for a death poem, but he refused them, claiming that in a sense every poem he had written in the last ten years—by far his most productive period and one of deep Zen involvement—had been done as if a death poem. Yet on the next morning his friends were called by the poet to his bedside and told that during the night he had dreamed, and that on waking a poem had come to him. Then he recited his famous poem:

> Sick, on a journey,
> Yet over withered fields
> Dreams wander on.

There are perhaps as many ways of dying, or at least of facing death, as there are of living, and though all death poems are compact, deep, intense, they reflect, as might be expected, the many differences to be found among men, including Zen masters. There is, for example, the serenity of Hofuku Seikatsu:

> Don't tell me how difficult the Way.
> The bird's path, winding far, is right
> Before you. Water of the Dokei Gorge,
> You return to the ocean, I to the mountain.

The power of Dogen:

> Four and fifty years
> I've hung the sky with stars.
> Now I leap through—
> What shattering!

The self-honesty of Keisen:

> The first illusion
> Has lasted seventy-six years.
> The final barrier?
> Three thousand sins!

In the case of enlightenment and death poems there are certain recognizable norms and standards, and it is possible to compare them for their concision and gravity, whatever the distinction of the poets. The general poems, as might be expected, are less easily judged, and cover a multitude of subjects, for in spite of the exigencies of the Zen life, not to speak of the expectations for him of others—to be ignored at peril, the Zen man finds himself moved to poetry by things not ostensibly associated with his discipline (though many general poems are so associated). As some have remarked, Zen art, be it the monochromic inkwash painting (*sumie*) long connected with Zen or poetry, is best characterized by its celebration of, its wonder at, the intimate relationship of all that exists in the world. Such feeling is, of course, not unknown in the West, and is beautifully expressed by Martin Buber:

Believe in the simple magic of life, in service in the universe, and the meaning of that waiting, that alertness, that "craning of the neck" in creatures, will dawn upon you. Every word would falsify; but look! round about you beings live their life, and to whatever point you turn you come upon being.

In Zen poetry the phenomenal world is never treated as mere setting for human actions; the drama is there, in nature, of which the human is an active part, in no way separated from his surroundings, neither contending with them, fearing them nor—for that matter—worshiping them. The Zennist is no pantheist: in order to feel at home in nature he does not find it necessary to imagine it as a godly immanence. Many of the general poems, then, express a simple awe at the beauty of the world:

Hearing the Snow

> This cold night bamboos stir,
> Their sound—now harsh, now soft—
> Sweeps through the lattice window.
> Though ear's no match for mind,
> What need, by lamplight,
> Of a single Scripture leaf?

—Kido

> Disciplined by wind and snow,
> The Way of Reinan opens.
> Look where—moon high, plums a-bloom—
> The temple's fixed in stillness.

—Eun

Though most of the general poems are written in the spirit of celebration, some are clearly meant to instruct or hearten the master's disciples, or as in the case of the following waka by Dogen, inspire those among the followers who might in moments of weakness question the purpose of what they are required to do:

Waka on Zen Sitting

Scarecrow in the hillock
Paddy field—
How unaware! How useful!

2

What have all Zen poems, of whatever type, in common and what distinguishes them from poems written by the artistic equals of the masters who work in other traditions, or independently? Takashi Ikemoto and I, interviewing for the volume *Zen: Poems, Prayers, Sermons, Anecdotes, Interviews* (New York, Doubleday, 1965), asked that question, as it relates to painting, of the Zen master Tenzan Yasuda. His reply:

What expresses cosmic truth in the most direct and concise way—that is the heart of Zen art. Please examine this picture ("Fisherman and Woodcutter" by Sesshu): of all the artist's pictures, this is my favorite. The boat at the fisherman's back tells us his occupation, the bundle of firewood behind the woodcutter tells his. The fisherman is drawn with only three strokes of the brush, the woodcutter with five. You couldn't ask for greater concision. And these two men, what are they talking about? In all probability, and this the atmosphere of the picture suggests, they are discussing something very important, something beneath the surface of daily life. How do I know? Why, every one of Sesshu's brush strokes tells me. . . . Western art has volume and richness when it is good. Yet to me it is too thickly encumbered by what is dispensable. It's as if the Western artist were trying to hide something, not reveal it.

Had the master been asked about haiku poetry or rock gardens or any of the other arts associated with Zen, he would have answered in a similar way, for its aesthetics are well and very subtly defined.

The four traditionally recognized dominant moods of Zen-related art are: Sabi, Wabi, Aware and Yugen. Often in large-scale works such as Noh plays, as the result of natural modulations, all the moods may be suggested, but in short literary works and in *sumie* painting the mood is clearly apparent. These moods are not consciously created, as in the case of Indian rasas (emotional "flavors" so precise that one rasa, say of a sitar melody, may "belong" to a particular time of the day and is always deliberately induced): they are experienced as we experience the light of the sky, hardly aware of the delicacy of its gradations.

Sabi may be defined as the feeling of isolation, or rather at a mid-point of the emotion when it is both welcome and unwelcome, source of both ease and unease. This mood, as all strong moods, comes as the result of many things, but clearly associated with Sabi is the sense of being detached, as in Honei's poem "Fisherman":

On wide waters, alone, my boat
Follows the current, deep/shallow, high/low.
Moved, I raise my flute to the moon,
Piercing the autumn sky.

Of importance to the mood of the poem is that in ancient China the fisherman, one of the so-called "four recluses" (the others being the farmer, the woodcutter and the herdsman), was held in great esteem by Taoists and Zennists. Hakuin, greatest of the Rinzai Zen masters of Japan, significantly titled a remarkable account of his spiritual progress *Yasenkanna*, which can be rendered as "talk in a boat at night."

Sabi is associated with the period of early monastic training, when if one is to succeed in Zen discipline a strong detachment must be cultivated. While in training the fifteenth-century Japanese master Saisho wrote as an interpretation of the koan on Joshu's Nothingness a poem the equal of Honei's in its spirit of Sabi:

Earth, mountains, rivers—hidden in this nothingness.
In this nothingness—earth, mountains, rivers revealed.
Spring flowers, winter snows:
There's no being nor non-being, nor denial itself.

Here the feeling of detachment is not only strong, it is identified as an essential precondition of enlightenment. Ch'ing-yuan's well-known words on the importance of *wu-hsin* (no-mind, detachment) will serve to paraphrase Saisho's poem:

Before I had studied Zen I saw mountains as mountains, waters as waters. When I learned something of Zen, the mountains were no longer mountains, waters no longer waters. But now that I understand Zen, I am at peace with myself, seeing mountains once again as mountains, waters as waters.

Wabi is the spirit of poverty, the poignant appreciation of what most consider the commonplace, and is associated in Zen with one of the principal characteristics, if not ideals, of the sect, an antirelativism: what's good? what's bad? what's valuable? valueless? The mood is perhaps most apparent in relation to that quintessential Zen art, the tea ceremony, which—from the utensils employed in the preparation of the tea to the very timber of the tea hut—is a celebration of the humble, the "handmade." The nineteenth-century haiku artist Masaoka Shiki writes:

> A thing long forgotten:
> Pot in which a flower blooms,
> This spring day.

Wabi is not to be found in objects alone. As in the following awakening poem by the sixteenth-century Japanese master Yuishun it is the feeling of something hitherto ignored suddenly being seen for the precious thing it is (and always has been, though hidden from us by illusion):

> Why, it's but the motion of eyes and brows!
> And here I've been seeking it far and wide.
> Awakened at last, I find the moon
> Above the pines, the river surging high.

One day while practicing zazen (formal sitting in meditation) with his followers the Chinese master Daibai was moved to say aloud for their benefit, "No suppressing arrival, no following departure." Immediately after the words were spoken the shriek of a weasel pierced through the meditation hall, and Daibai recited this extemporaneous poem:

> I'm at one with this, *this* only.
> You, my disciples,
> Uphold it firmly—
> Now I can breathe my last.

To know what Daibai meant by asking his followers to "uphold" the simple fact of the weasel's shriek is to appreciate the importance of Wabi to Zen. How much more real, how much more relevant to the spiritual quest than even the wisest words is Nature's least manifestation, when accepted for the profound thing it is.

Aware is the sadness that comes with the sense of the impermanence of things, the realization that they are lost to us even as they are found. It is so constant a mood in the poetry touched by Buddhism that as far back as the tenth century, when the Japanese poet Ki no Tsurayuki (died 946) compiled the anthology *Kokinshu*, the first done under Imperial order, he could write:

> When these poets saw the scattered spring blossoms, when they heard leaves falling in the autumn evening, when they saw reflected in their mirrors the snow and the waves of each passing year, when they were stunned into an awareness of the brevity of life by the dew on the grass or foam on the water . . . they were inspired to write poems.

A few centuries later Kenko Yoshida, a famous poet and court official of his day who became a Buddhist monk in 1324, wrote in his *Essays in Idleness*:

> If we lived forever, if the dews of Adashino never vanished, the crematory smoke on Toribeyama never faded, men would hardly feel the pity of things. The beauty of life is in its impermanence. Man lives the longest of all living things—consider the ephemera, the cicada—, and even one year lived peacefully seems very long. Yet for such as love the world, a thousand years would fade like the dream of one night.

At times the sense of Aware is so powerful that the only way of coming to terms with it is to identify with it totally, perhaps retiring from the world and the constant reminders of its limited, conditioned nature. Many of the finest Zen poems, seemingly "escapist," have this spirit of acceptance, of oneness with what *is*, whatever it happens to be. Here is the fourteenth-century Japanese master Jakushitsu:

Refreshing, the wind against the waterfall
As the moon hangs, a lantern, on the peak
And the bamboo window glows. In old age mountains
Are more beautiful than ever. My resolve:
That these bones be purified by rocks.

And here the Chinese master Zotan is seen praising a fellow monk "Shooku" (Woodcutter's Hut), whose retirement very much impressed him:

Is the live branch better than the dead?
Cut through each—what difference?
Back home, desires quelled, you sit by
The half-closed brushwood door the spring day through.

It is perhaps in haiku poetry that Aware is most keenly felt, though because it is so commonly suggested (*Sunt lacrimae rerum*—There are tears for things) it is the spoiler of many otherwise acceptable verses. But by those who care for haiku the sentimental is never mistaken for the poignant, and a piece like the following by Yosa Buson (1715–83), important Nanga-style painter as well as poet, is greatly prized:

I feel a sudden chill—
In our bedroom, my dead wife's comb,
Underfoot.

Yugen, most difficult of the dominant moods to describe, is the sense of a mysterious depth in all that makes up nature. Often the term is used in almost a purely aesthetic way, as in the theoretical writings on Noh theater by the most important figure in its development, Zeami (1363–1443). In his essay "On Attaining the Stage of Yugen" he speaks of the mood as that which "marks supreme attainment in all the arts and accomplishments" and describes its essence as "true beauty and gentleness," a "realm of tranquillity and elegance." Though such may be the effect of Yugen on the Noh stage, perhaps a better sense of what the mood can represent in Zen is suggested by these words of the contemporary Japanese Soto master Rosen Takashina:

The true basis of the universe is stillness, its real condition, for out of it comes all activity. The ocean, when the wind ceases, is calm again, as are the trees and grasses. These things return to stillness, their natural way. And this is the principle of meditation. There is night, there is day, when the sun sets there is a hush, and then the dead of night, when all is still. This is the meditation of nature.

Yugen is the sense of the mystic calm in things (in T. S. Eliot's phrase, in "Burnt Norton," "the still point of the turning world"), which is always there, below the surface, but which reveals itself only to the "ready."

Etsuzan, the Chinese master, aware that his time was nearly up, looked into things as never before, and wrote:

> Light dies in the eyes, hearing
> Fades. Once back to the Source,
> There's no special meaning—
> Today, tomorrow.

For him the world had returned to a stillness, its natural condition, and perhaps the realization gave him comfort in his final hour. Yugen also suggests the sense of a strong communion with nature, a descent into depths, as in this poem by the seventeenth-century Japanese master Manan:

> Unfettered at last, a traveling monk,
> I pass the old Zen barrier.
> Mine is a traceless stream-and-cloud life.
> Of those mountains, which shall be my home?

And in this poem, one of his most famous, by Dogen:

> This slowly drifting cloud is pitiful;
> What dreamwalkers men become.
> Awakened, I hear the one true thing—
> Black rain on the roof of Fukakusa Temple.

To hear that "black rain" with Dogen, to sense that it—or anything like it, for though intensely particular it is symbolic—is the "one true thing" is to enter the realm of Yugen, which as a mood is not of course peculiar to Zen but which, nonetheless, is most commonly felt in its art. Not to hear it, on the other hand, not to know if one hears that one has identified with the Source is to remain a "dreamwalker," blind not only to the beauty of the world but to its reality.

The four dominant moods, however closely associated with Zen art, are not exclusively related to the philosophy, whereas *zenki*, the sense of a spontaneous activity outside the established forms, as if flowing from the formless self, is the constant in its art. Without Zen there could not be *zenki*, just as without *muga* (so close an identification of subject and object that "self" disappears) the goal of Zen, satori, could not be realized. There have been occasional attempts to describe in detail the characteristics of Zen art, the most comprehensive being Dr. Hisamatsu's in *Zen and Fine Arts*, which gives as its chief qualities the following (all of which, according to Dr. Hisamatsu, are present harmoniously in every Zen work, whatever the medium): asymmetry, simplicity, freedom, naturalness, profundity, unworldliness and stillness.

It is perhaps in poetry that these characteristics—subject and theme dictating to what degree, of course—are most apparent, the desired qualities of an aesthetic. The following three poems have a common theme, and each in its way might be seen as representing the ideal Zen poem in Japan. The first is by the thirteenth-century master Unoku:

> Moving/resting is meaningless.
> Traceless, leaving/coming.
> Across moonlit mountains,
> Howling wind!

And here is one by the fourteenth-century master Getsudo:

> The perfect way out:
> There's no past/present/future.
> Dawn after dawn, the sun!
> Night after night, the moon!

And now one by the contemporary Shinkichi Takahashi, "Wind Among the Pines":

> The wind blows hard among the pines
> Toward the beginning
> Of an endless past.
> Listen: you've heard everything.

Against the facts of that wind, that sun, that moon, what are concepts such as time? these poems seem to be asking. And as in all genuine Zen art, calm replaces restlessness.

In Zen painting there are only the essential strokes, the space surrounding them being filled in by the mind, which poises itself on (imagines) what it knows best, that which is always tranquil, agreeable. The brush strokes, however few, serve to make the mind aware of the space, suggested not so much by the absence of objects but by the manner in which the objects are absorbed. And in poetry perhaps the most important things are to be found in the silence following the words, for it is then that the reader or listener becomes conscious of the calm within. It is something felt, not known, and precious in the way that only the spiritual can be.

3

There are distinct types of Zen poetry, and distinguishing qualities, but what makes it unique in world literature is that it is recognized as a mystic Way—to a most difficult truth. Zen has other Ways (dō) but Kadō, the Way of poetry, is one that has always held a place of honor in its culture, which has always valued directness, concision and forcefulness of expression. As Dr. D. T. Suzuki writes in one of his essays, "The Meditation Hall":

> The Zen masters, whenever they could, avoided the technical nomenclature of Buddhist philosophy; not only did they discuss such subjects as appealed to a plain man, but they made use of his everyday language. . . . Thus Zen literature became a unique repository of ancient wisdom . . . [refusing] to express itself in the worn-out, lifeless language of scholars. . . .

The masters also discouraged the dependence on scriptural writings, and a master like Tokusan could proclaim (in one of the stories of the *Mumonkan* [Barrier Without Gate], an early thirteenth-century classic of Chinese Zen): "However deep your knowledge of the scriptures, it is no more than a strand of hair in the vastness of space; however important seeming your worldly experience, it is but a drop of water in a deep ravine." And as the fourteenth-century Japanese master Shutaku wrote:

> Mind set free in the Dharma-realm,
> I sit at the moon-filled window
> Watching the mountains with my ears,
> Hearing the stream with open eyes.
> Each molecule preaches perfect law,
> Each moment chants true sutra:
> The most fleeting thought is timeless,
> A single hair's enough to stir the sea.

While discouraging dependence on scripture (sutra learning), the masters strongly encouraged the cultivation of non-attachment, upheld by all the sects of Buddhism, the ultimate aim of whose discipline was, quoting from Dr. Suzuki again, "to release the spirit from its possible bondage so that it could act freely in accordance with its own principles—that is what is meant by non-attachment."

To give some idea of the manner in which such an important ideal, one with scriptural authority, is dealt with by Zennists, here is the Japanese master Takuan (1573-1645) in a "Letter to the Shogun's Fencing Master":

If your mind is fixed on a certain spot, it will be seized by that spot and no activities can be performed efficiently. Not to fix your mind anywhere is essential. Not fixed anywhere, the mind is everywhere. . . . The Original Mind is like water which flows freely . . . whereas the deluded mind is like ice. . . . There is a passage [in the *Diamond Sutra*] that says: "The mind should operate without abiding anywhere."

Presumably dissatisfied with his explanation, Takuan goes on:

It is like tying a cat with a rope to prevent it from catching a baby sparrow which is tied up nearby. If your mind is tied down by a rope as is the cat, your mind cannot function properly. It is better to train the cat not to harm the sparrow when they are together, so that it can be free to move anywhere. . . . That is the meaning of the passage [in the *Diamond Sutra*]. . . .

How bumbling and obvious when compared with the poem Takuan was to write on the theme some time later:

> Though night after night
> The moon is stream-reflected,
> Try to find where it has touched,
> Point even to a shadow.

Which is perhaps the equal of Dogen's poem on the same passage in the *Diamond Sutra*:

Coming, going, the waterfowl
Leaves not a trace,
Nor does it need a guide.

And resembles the eighteenth-century master Sogyo's:

Careful! Even moonlit dewdrops,
If you're lured to watch,
Are a wall before the truth.

And the contemporary Japanese Zen poet Shinkichi Takahashi's "Fish":

I hold a newspaper, reading.
Suddenly my hands become cow ears,
Then turn into Pusan, the South Korean port.

Lying on a mat
Spread on the bankside stones,
I fell asleep.
But a willow leaf, breeze-stirred,
Brushed my ear.
I remained just as I was,
Near the murmurous water.

When young there was a girl
Who became a fish for me.
Whenever I wanted fish
Broiled in salt, I'd summon her.
She'd get down on her stomach
To be sun-cooked on the stones.
And she was always ready!

Alas, she no longer comes to me.
An old benighted drake,
I hobble homeward.
But look, my drake feet become horse hoofs!
Now they drop off
And, stretching marvelously,
Become the tracks of the Tokaido Railway Line.

Thus an important Buddhist principle, first advanced by scripture, often quoted and allegorized by masters (as in Takuan's "Letter . . ." or Hyakujo Ekai's famous injunction, *Fujaku fugu*—No clinging, no seeking), is transmuted into superb poetry by men who not only know truth but feel.

We have examined the nature of the three main types of Zen poetry, its characteristics, and have shown the manner in which it expresses insights afforded by the philosophy. Perhaps from our discussion something like a viewpoint has emerged, namely that if one wishes to "understand" Zen Buddhism, one could do worse than go to its arts, especially the poetry, compared with which the many disquisitions on its meaning are as dust to living earth. We see in these poems, as in all important religious art, East or West, revelations of spiritual truths touched by a kind of divinity.

Lucien Stryk

London, England
February 1973

ZEN POEMS OF CHINA AND JAPAN
THE CRANE'S BILL

CHINA

ENLIGHTENMENT

1

The mountain slopes crawl with lumberjacks,
Axing everything in sight—
Yet crimson flowers
Burn along the stream.

—Chin-doba, ?

2

Rolling the bamboo blind, I
Look out at the world—what change!
Should someone ask what I've discovered,
I'll smash this whisk against his mouth.

—Chokei, d. 932

3

All's harmony, yet everything is separate.
Once confirmed, mastery is yours.
Long I hovered on the Middle Way,
Today the very ice shoots flame.

—Chokei

4

Nansen said: It's everywhere.
Today, here at home, I'm through the Gate!
It seems just everything's a dear old grandpa.
The good grandchild, turning, burns with shame.

—Chosha, 9 c.

5

Every thing, every place is real,
Each particle makes up Original Man.
Still, the absolutely real is voiceless,
The true body's majestically out of sight.

—Chosha

6

Light everywhere, I live in all.
Avoiding thought, All appears.
Yet should one of the six senses stir,
Clouds gather. Delusion? Satori?
Forget them. Follow the Law, all's well.
Nirvana? Samsara? Airy flowers both.

—Chosetsu, 9 c.

7

I was born with a divine jewel,
Long since filmed with dust.
This morning, wiped clean, it mirrors
Streams and mountains, without end.

—Ikuzanchu, ?

8

Does one really have to fret
About enlightenment?
No matter what road I travel,
I'm going home.

—Shinsho, ?

9

"From the very beginning
All things are in nirvana"—
Here's spring with its hundred blossoms,
A yellow warbler at song in the willow.

—Anonymous

10

The day the Emperor treated me
In Zephyr Hall, my eyes shot wide:
It isn't true the Mystery
Of Futsu journeyed over Sorei Range.

—Etsuzan, 10 c.

11

Meeting Master Oryu taught me this:
Your mind can make you ill.
Harp smashed, gourd and bag tossed,
No longer do I dig for gold in amalgams.

—Rodohin, 10 c.

12

When Master Ungo asked,
"What is it comes?" I danced for joy.
Though one grasps it on the spot,
One's still buried alive.

—Zuigan, 10 c.

13

I'm twenty-seven years
And always sought the Way.
Well, this morning we passed
Like strangers on the road.

—Kokuin, 10 c.

14

Iron will's demanded of
The student of the Way—
It's always on the mind.
Forget all—good, bad.
Suddenly it's yours.

—Rijunkyoku, 11 c.

15

The stone mortar rushes through the air,
The golden lion turns into a dog.
Is it the North Star you reach for?
Fold hands behind the South.

—Yooku, ?

Twenty-odd years in doubt—
How many times I've stirred the mind-ash.
Now, refined, I've met an old
Acquaintance. What a genius was Li Po!

—Joju, 11 c.

For thirty-eight years totally unaware,
Now I've gained it. What difference?
The rushing Ben River, the broad Zui banks.
Arrow-waves are shooting east. I'm going home.

—Ritangen, 11 c.

Until today the precious gem's been buried,
Now it flashes from the earth. Mind's clear
At last. Zen-sitting, a stick of incense
Lights the universe. I bow to Bodhidharma.

—Ryozan, 10 c.

19

Arms stretching from the precipice, finally
I'm free. Horizon's flat now, the ravine's
Lit up without the moon. On the hermitage
Gate hangs a luminous bamboo screen.

—Koseisoku, 12 c.

20

This grasped, all's dust—
The sermon for today.
Lands, seas. Awakened,
You walk the earth alone.

—Seigensai, 12 c.

21

One who rises, rises of himself,
One who falls, falls from himself.
Autumn dew, spring breeze—
Nothing can possibly interfere.

—Ni-buttsu, 12 c.

22

Forget everything—everything!
Now from the path the night bell
Tinkling. Is that the moon
At the bottom of the pool?
The mud bull shatters against the coral.

—Tosu, 12 c.

23

One-two-three-four-five-six-seven,
On one foot I tip the dizzy peak.
I seize the jewel from the dragon's jaw,
Outwitting Vimalakirti, just like that.

—Ten-i, 11 c.

24

There I was, hunched over office desk,
Mind an unruffled pool.
A thunderbolt! My middle eye
Shot wide, revealing—my ordinary self.

—Layman Seiken, 11 c.

25

With one foot on the brick step,
The All burst in my head.
I had a good laugh by
The box tree, moon in the bluest sky.

—Choro, 11 c.

26

Fathomed at last!
Ocean's dried, Void burst.
Without an obstacle in sight,
It's everywhere!

—Joho, 12 c.

27

One question, and master thunders.
Mount Sumeru hides in the Big Dipper,
Billows cover the very sky.
Here's a nose. A mouth.

—Kyochu, 12 c.

28

Frogs croak in moonlight,
Heaven, earth sliced through—all
One. Yet who understands?
Upon the mountain, Gensha's bleeding foot.

—Layman Chokyusei, 12 c.

29

The great poisoned drum
Quakes earth, heaven.
Turn back, look—
Dead bodies miles around.

—Myotan, 1176–1247

DEATH

30

Don't tell me how difficult the Way.
The bird's path, winding far, is right
Before you. Water of the Dokei Gorge,
You return to the ocean, I to the mountain.

          —Hofuku Seikatsu, 10 c.

31

Eighty-eight, my head's pure white.
Peacefully I governed Double Peak Mountain,
A moon glowing over a thousand waters.
High on Yellow Plum Mount I received
The Patriarch's word, on White Omen Mount
The secrets of the sect. Daily I enjoin
Disciples: tend well the flame of the Law.

          —Seiko, 10 c.

32

Maitreya! Maitreya!
Forever dividing himself,
He's here, there, everywhere—
Yet scarcely noticed.

—Hotei, d. 917

33

From the start there's no
Life and death, yet I've gained
The leaving/staying mind.
In the next life I'll probably return.

—Sensai, d. 657

34

How long the stars
Have been fading,
Lamplight dimming:
There's neither coming,
Nor going.

—Nansen, 748–834

35

I'm at one with this, *this* only.
You, my disciples,
Uphold it firmly—
Now I can breathe my last.

—Daibai, 8 c.

36

For eighty years I've talked of east and west:
What nonsense. What's long/short? big/small?
There's no need of the gray old man, I'm one
With all of you, in everything. Once through
The emptiness of all, who's coming? Who going?

—Kiyo, 8 c.

37

All Patriarchs are above our understanding,
And they don't last forever.
O my disciples, examine, examine.
What? Why this. This only.

—Beirei, 8 c.

38

Lifting hands, I climb the South Star,
Then turn to lean against the North.
Step beyond the sky, look—
Where is there another like myself?

—Godai Chitsu, 9 c.

39

I've remained in Mokuchin thirty years.
In all that time not one disciplinary merit.
If asked why Bodhidharma came from the West
I'll say, unknitting my brow—"What's that?"

—Mokuchin Juro, 9 c.

40

This year turning sixty-four, elements
About to dissolve within me—the Path!
A miracle of miracles, yet where
The Buddhas and Patriarchs? No need
To shave my head again, or wash.
Just set the firewood flaming—that's enough.

—Nangaku Gentai, 9 c.

41

Escaping the world, I became a priest,
My master prescribing total calm.
Thirty years on this mountain with disciples,
My principle unchanged: only the most
Discreet portioning, of everything.
Understand? Listen well before I close my eyes.

—Ryuko, 9 c.

42

Hands released, I twirl the letter-board.
Just in time, I push aside my mat.
Clouds break up, the river roars,
Yet calm as ever, empty heaven, empty earth.

—Tenneimyo, ?

43

Light dies in the eyes, hearing
Fades. Once back to the Source,
There's no special meaning—
Today, tomorrow.

—Etsuzan, 10 c.

44

I've reached my seventy-seventh year.
Today things are no less impermanent
Than ever. The sun in its meridian,
I bend knees with both hands.

—Gyozan, 840–916

45

Leaving, where to go? Staying, where?
Which to choose? I stand aloof.
To whom speak my parting words? The galaxy,
White, immense. A crescent moon.

—Shoten, 11 c.

46

Silvery world, golden body—
Animate, inanimate are one.
Light and dark expended, nothing shines.
And yet—the sun!

—Shuzan, 926–993

47

At ninety-nine, snowy side-locks,
Beard, a thin-shouldered, fur-robed one
Has cut all earthly ties. Laughing, I point
To the swift clouds. Jewel Hare blazes over all.

—Gen of Kohoin, d. 1085

48

The Mount Sumeru mallet firmly gripped,
I pound through the drum of space.
Hiding, I leave not a trace—
Behold the snared sun!

—Shonen, 1215–89

49

I've stalked the world,
Awing Buddhas, Patriarchs.
Arrow flashing,
What's earth? What's sky?

—Issan, 1247–1317

50

Sixty-nine years:
Birth/death, birth/death.
Clouds no longer cover
The old ford, water's sky-blue.

—Tomei, 1272–1340

GENERAL

51

In all of earth and heaven
There's not room enough for a stick—
The blissful Void. Welcome the three-foot
Sword of Gen, lightning through the breeze.

—Sogen, 1226–86

52

FLUTIST DIVINER

Who nowadays hears the ancient tune of Ji Peak?
Master diviner of our destiny, do you?
A, B, C, D, E, F, G—
"Spring Time," "White Snow," "Song of the Partridge."

—Daisen, 13 c.

53

FISHERMAN

On wide waters, alone, my boat
Follows the current, deep/shallow, high/low.
Moved, I raise my flute to the moon,
Piercing the autumn sky.

—Honei, 11 c.

54

FISHERMAN

Spring light, soft bank mist,
And on the still water his boat.
He grips in his dream a thousand-foot line,
Match for the greatest whale.

—Setcho, 980–1052

THE DREAM PALACE

The grand Dream Palace, six windows shut—
How refreshing the breeze across my pillow.
Such have always been Buddhas and Patriarchs.
Peals from the belfry—I listen to each.

—Kaiseki, 13 c.

A restless mind, all night,
And now the shriek of monkeys!
Down in the temple, at the foot of
Transplant Peak, how many broken hearts?

—Kaiseki

57

TO A MONK DEPARTING FOR MID STREAM

Over Dragon Pool frozen clouds
Make sleep impossible. I've heard
The woodcutter's song: you're welcome to it.
It will never reach those boats.

—Seigan, 1198–1262

58

ON SEEING LUTE PRIEST OFF

Achieving perfection beyond the thirteen notes,
Your harmony's your very own.
Go now, playing not even "The Crane's Hatred."
Pines surge outside my gate.

—Enkei, 1189–1263

59

MONK FROM ETSU RETURNING TO A
HERMITAGE

His dreams are ranged with the mountains of Etsu,
Unforgettable his nirvana-grasp on Vulture Peak.
In the small hours monkeys cry in the moon,
Then bells from the Monastery Tower.

—Enkei

60

HEARING THE SNOW

This cold night bamboos stir,
Their sound—now harsh, now soft—
Sweeps through the lattice window.
Though ear's no match for mind,
What need, by lamplight,
Of a single Scripture leaf?

—Kido, 1185–1269

61

THE YOMYO STUPA

Before the gate, served up on a platter,
The long lake mirror.
Who says Yomyo is verbose? Wine's
Mellowness isn't in the quaffing.

—Zotan, 13 c.

62

WOODCUTTER'S HUT

Is the live branch better than the dead?
Cut through each—what difference?
Back home, desires quelled, you sit by
The half-closed brushwood door the spring day through.

—Zotan

63

With no-mind I've enjoyed my stay,
With mind I return to So, my homeland.
Whether in mind or not,
I'm content en route to Heaven.

—Gotsuan, d. 1276

64

My sacred sword's invisible:
Let go, it's light as straw,
Gripped, it jets with flame.
Protecting me these years,
It showed itself today—
Let Mara's army come!

—Ingen, 1592–1673

65

MASTER SUIAN'S BIRTHPLACE

Out shot Master Suian's fist,
Temple crashing round his ears.
The old tiller, unaware, whips
His ox across the paddy field.

—Sekirin, 13 c.

66

CROSSING THE SENTO RIVER

Paddling misty straits mid Go and Etsu,
Blue peaks tumbling either bank,
The boat rolls on—yet how compare
These surges with the heart of man?

—Masso, 13 c.

67

FROGS CROAKING

Lichen-crusted frogs croak
At moonlit mountaintops.
Awakened, mind's clear at last.
Refreshing pine winds
Of the *Book of Songs*
Can't match *this*.

—Masso

68

LISTENING TO THE LUTE

Perfect melody—like wind
Among the pines of far-off slopes.
Mind's washed sky clean:
Hear it beyond itself.

—Jakuan, 12 c.

69

FLYING SNOW ROCK

The thousand-foot snow dragon
Sails down from the sky,
Lighting the glazed ravine.
Should it appear in summer,
Toss your silk-gauze gown!

—Zetsuzo, 13 c.

70

DRIED BONES UNDER THE PINE

Bones in the grass beneath the dream body.
Thought, feeling spent, the Truth is out.
Now in the raw-food season,
On Hokubo's path, spring's on the pine.

—Etsudo, 13 c.

71

A vegetarian in shabby robe, my spirit's
Like the harvest moon—free, life through.
Asked where I dwell, I'll say:
In green water, on the blue mountain.

—Ryuge, 835–923

72

One room, one bed—enough.
One jar, one bowl.
A road runs to the village,
There's not a house I know.

—Ryuge

73

Mind, mind, mind—above the Path.
Here on my mountain, gray hair down,
I cherish bamboo sprouts, brush carefully
By pine twigs. Burning incense,
I open a book: mist over flagstones.
Rolling the blind, I contemplate:
Moon in the pond. Of my old friends,
How many know the Way?

—Zengetsu, 833–912

74

LIVING IN THE MOUNTAINS (1)

What good's world—profit, fame?
Halfway down the path of scarlet mist,
Travelers worry over graying hair,
Cold winds remind them how alone
They are. At sunset, cicada's song.
Who'd take the hermit farther,
By deep waters, under thick clouds?

—Sen of Kyuho, 10 c.

75

LIVING IN THE MOUNTAINS (2)

It's not easy to live in the mountains.
Prattling their ignorance, envying
My life under moonlit clouds, rainy wind.
Where paths snake through the rocky valley,
My discipline's not all that much.

—Sen of Kyuho

JAPAN

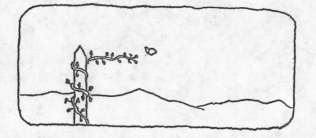

ENLIGHTENMENT

76

Satori seekers make me sick!
Those that find it are deluded.
The old gimlet on Vulture Mountain—laughable.
Over my shoulder flies the broken ladle.

                   —Kakua, 12 c.

77

I've crossed the sea after Truth.
Knowledge, that snare, must be defied.
Here and there, I've worn out heaps of sandals.
Now—moonlit water in the clear abyss.

                   —Kakua

78

Forgetting mind, its complications,
My hand is free. The All appears.
I use devices, simultaneously.
Look—a halo penetrates the Void.

—Kakua

79

How can I tell what I've seen?
Fall, stand—it's clear at once.
Wearing my cowl backwards, I
Trample the old path. And the new.

—Kakua

80

Fisting, shouting like a petty merchant,
Saying yes, no: quicksand.
Cease pointing, explaining. Keep quiet.
There: now hear the flutist coming home?

—Kakua

81

With one stroke I rammed the demon's den,
Smashing Nada's furious iron face.
My ears are deaf, mouth dumb—
Touch it, stars shoot everywhere.

—Sogen, 13 c.

82

No longer aware of mind and object,
I see earth, mountains, rivers at last.
The Dharmakaya's everywhere.
Worldlings, facing it, can't make it out.

—Daio, 1235–1308

83

Not seeing that a "Zen man" is no Zen man,
I was a lump of doubt for twenty years—
Kozan's poisoned drum destroyed at last,
Earth and heaven soar like Mount Sumeru.

—Guchu, 1334–1409

84

For twenty years I've sought the Other.
Now, letting go, I fly out of the pit.
What use oneness of mind and body?
These days I only sing la-la-la.

—Keso Shogaku, 15 c.

85

Original Face is the reality of realities:
Stretch your hand to the winging bird.
Vertical nose, horizontal eyes—and then?
What if your mind *is* empty?

—Tokugaku, 15 c.

86

Who said the sea's concave,
Mountains convex?
Why, I swallow them whole—
The boneless sky!

—Heishin, 1287–1369

87

Straw sandals worn through, soles blistered.
Reaching home, I'd bathe my feet, then snooze.
Always I'd weep, uncertain, at the crossroads.
This morning, an awakening—the flaming lotus!

—Taiko, 1233–1321

88

Unmon's barrier pulled down, the old
Path lost. Blue sky's my home,
My every action beyond men's reach:
A golden priest, arms folded, has returned.

                    —Daito, 1282–1337

89

I've swallowed the Eastern Ocean's iron ball—
How dark the universe of three thousand things.
Mother-born eyes plucked out at last,
Look, I hold high the broken bowl.

                    —Giten, 1396–1465

90

Glittering sky: thirty blows of the staff!
Now earth is black. Since last night
I've hugged the open window:
Ivy-twined moon, pine wind: I'm frozen to the marrow.

—Toin, 15 c.

91

Any moment now I'll knock my master down:
A single blow's enough to flatten five Sumeru Mounts.
Awe-inspiring, I fill earth and heaven
When, as now, I bow thrice to my master.

—Keisen, 1425–1500

92

I flung open all six windows on the moon.
Unju only scolded, "Dust in the eye!"
Gem crushed in my hand, I held
A lump of iron.

—Bassui, 1327–57

93

Flint spark? Lightning? All too late.
A timely *kwatz* crushes Mount Sumeru.
Yet I've a body-turning word:
Place bowl on the *tan*, fall to.

—Gokei, 1416–1500

94

Awakened under stick and *kwatz*,
I was driven by the karma wind
Into Iron Mountain. Patriarchs
Have nowhere else to go.
This morning we returned, hand in hand.

—Hakutei, 1437–1527

95

Kwatz too weak, stick too short,
I've kneaded the universe to an abode.
Spring at the capital is out in peonies.
Laughing, clapping hands, I came back home.

—Seisen, 15 c.

96

Mind and object scrapped,
I move beyond plains, mountains, streams.
Dharmakaya's everywhere—
Yet worldlings stand about stone-blind.

—Daio, 1235–1308

DEATH

97

Four and fifty years
I've hung the sky with stars.
Now I leap through—
What shattering!

—Dogen, 1200–53

98

Fifty-six years, above Buddhas, Patriarchs,
I've stood mid-air.
Now I announce my final journey—
Daily sun breaks from the eastern ridge.

—Doyu, 1201–56

99

These eighty-four years,
Still, astir, Zen's been mine.
My last word?
Spoken before time began.

—Kangan, 1217–1300

100

One thousand and one tumbles,
Ninety-one years through.
Snow covers reeds for miles,
Full in the midnight sky, the moon.

—Tettsu, 1219–1309

101

For eighty-seven years
A bubble on the sea,
Windless, waveless,
Waveless, windless still.

—Muju, 1226–1312

102

What's life? What's death?
I blast the Void.
Winds spring up
In every quarter.

—Yuzan, 1301–70

103

Seventy-seven long years
I've reviled the Scriptures,
Zen itself. A failure through
And through, I piss on Brahma.

—Isan, 1795–1864

104

South of Mount Sumeru
Who understands my Zen?
Call Master Kido over—
He's not worth a cent.

—Ikkyu, 1394–1481

I've walked the world over:
Buddhas and Patriarchs engulfed.
The arrow twanged, sky
Topples to the earth.

—Issan, 1247–1317

Moving/resting is meaningless.
Traceless, leaving/coming.
Across moonlit mountains,
Howling wind!

—Unoku, 1248–1321

107

Ask Buddha—he doesn't know.
Nor do Patriarchs.
Beyond our grasp:
Who was born? Who died?

—Unzan, ?

108

Death sitting, death standing—
Bone-heap on the earth.
Void somersaults in the wind—
One final *kwatz!*

—Koho, 1241-1316

109

Abusing Scripture, cursing Zen,
I'm in my eighty-first year.
As earth and heaven crumble, I plunge
To the blazing fountain underground.

—Giun, 1253–1333

110

Coming and going, life and death:
A thousand hamlets, a million houses.
Don't you get the point?
Moon in the water, blossom in the sky.

—Gizan, 1802–78

111

Coming, I don't enter at the gate,
Going, I don't leave by the door.
This very body
Is the land of tranquil light.

—Gyokko, 1315–95

112

Life—not coming.
Death—not returning.
Where there are masterly feats,
The blind donkey hears thunder.

—Gyokuchu, 1522–1604

113

The first illusion
Has lasted seventy-six years.
The final barrier?
Three thousand sins!

—Keisen, 1425–1500

114

Drop by drop, seventy-seven winters,
Water's turned to ice.
Now this miraculous stroke—
I draw water from the flaming fount.

—Keso, 1352–1428

115

The perfect way out:
There's no past/present/future.
Dawn after dawn, the sun!
Night after night, the moon!

                         —Getsudo, 1285–1361

116

For seventy-four years
I've touched east, west.
My parting word?
Listen—I'll whisper.

                         —Kokan, 1770–1843

117

The difficult road:
No coming, no going.
Ask where I dwell?
The mud-ox bellows.

—Kokuo, 13 c.

118

A numskull for eighty-five years!
At last, swinging the body over,
I smite the blue sky.

—Kogetsu, 1668–1752

119

Life and death? Shoving a cart
Against a wall. I've pulverized
Mount Sumeru—in the whole
Cosmos-ocean not a trace of wind.

—Jittei, d. 1423

120

Arrival/departure: what difference?
Non-dependent, I go off alone.
Moonlight overspreads the earth.

—Sanso, 1232–1301

121

Fifty-four years I've entered
Horses, donkeys, saving limitless beings.
Now, farewell, farewell!
And don't forget—apply yourselves.

—Jisso, 1851–1904

122

Unaware of coming, going,
I turn back alone.
Caught in the midnight sky,
The moon silvering all.

—Eun, 1232–1301

123

I tongue-lashed wind and rain,
Above Buddhas, Patriarchs.
Lightning's no match for mind.

—Daio, 1235–1308

124

Seventy-six years,
Unborn, undying:
Clouds break up,
Moon sails on.

—Tokken, 1244–1319

125

I've plowed and sown my field,
Bought, sold. Yet it's ever new,
The young plants burgeoning.
In Buddha Hall a tiller, hoe in hand.

—Keizan, 1268–1325

GENERAL

126

Firm on the seven Buddhas' cushion,
Center, center. Here's the armrest
My master handed down. Now, to it!
Head up, eyes straight, ears in line with shoulders.

—Dogen, 1200–53

127

WAKA ON THE CORRECT-LAW EYE
TREASURY

There in midnight water,
Waveless, windless,
The old boat's swamped
With moonlight.

—Dogen

128

WAKA

Mind's no solid
One can touch or see—
Dew, frost.

—Dogen

129

WAKA ON ZEN SITTING

Scarecrow in the hillock
Paddy field—
How unaware! How useful!

—Dogen

130

WAKA ON IMPERMANENCE

The world? Moonlit
Drops shaken
From the crane's bill.

— Dogen

131

WAKA ON KYOSEI'S RAINDROP SOUND

As he listened,
Mindlessly,
The eavesdrops entered him.

— Dogen

132

I'm but a festering lump,
Most bestial of humans.
Years I've walked Chinese fashion,
Barefoot. Straw sandals
Brand-new, I touch my nose.

—Ejo, 1198–1280

133

Saddled as everyone with karma,
Who can deny the Buddha-mind within?
Ever yoked, yet not a glimpse of him.
At last I've tracked him down: myself.

—Tettsu, 1219–1309

134

WAKA

There among the plum twigs,
Dry yet blooming,
The oriole's silent song!

—Anonymous

135

SENRYU

Sitting back on both
Good and bad reed,
I taste the evening cool.

—Hakuin, 1685–1768

136

ON WISDOM

Ears deaf, eyes blind: Void's
Disembodied, nightly.
Shariputra tries but can't
Grasp wisdom. A lame Persian
Crossing just another ferry.

—Hakuin

137

Eyes blinded by three poisons,
Yet once all ties are cut,
How restful. Wicker hat donned,
Cane held firm, how vast the sky!

—Ungo, 1583–1659

138

Careful? Even moonlit dewdrops,
If you're lured to watch,
Are a wall before the Truth.

—Sogyo, 1667–1731

139

Eighty years, a day's journey.
I've lived everywhere, and now
The spring breeze doesn't try my door.
Snow lies heavy on my head.

—Guan, 18 c.

140

Sea touches sky, and now, moon down,
Waves are mirrors once again.
Through the still night, songs from small boats,
People stirring at their windows.

—Getsuo, d. 1342

141

CROSSING LAKE BIWA

Riding rain, astride wind, my plain robe light,
For ten *ri* the boat carries me across.
Hoisting sail, one knows how strong the wind.
The current tries both stem and stern.
Above the lake, mountains everywhere, among
The waves, in all directions, phantom paths.
A monk on a reed boat? And this not Futsu?
Ridiculous! Where is my Buddha-mind?

—Geppa, b. 1664

142

Disciplined by wind and snow,
The Way of Reinan opens.
Look where—moon high, plums a-bloom—
The temple's fixed in stillness.

—Eun, 1232–1301

143

Who's aware of mutability?
Not even Buddhas, Patriarchs.
What's tipping the peak
On one foot, head three feet long?

—Daitetsu, 1333–1408

144

WAKA ON SEEING AND HEARING DIRECTLY

Remain apart,
The world's yours—
A Buddha in the flesh.

—Bunan, 1602–76

145

TO ONE WHO REVERES BUDDHISM

The Law: unchain
The mind from all.
Still, mind
Is chained to Law.

—Bunan

146

TO ONE WHO HANKERS AFTER
BUDDHAHOOD

Don't fancy for a moment,
Though you pitch head
Over heels to Hell,
That you'll become a Buddha.

—Bunan

147

Mugo's life cry: "Don't be
Hoodwinked!" Zuigan's: "My master!"
Napping by the sunny ivied window,
I'm only roused by mountain pines.

—Jakushitsu, 1290–1367

148

Right's fine, wrong's fine—
There's nothing to nirvana,
And what's "defilement"?
Snowflake in the flame.

—Gudo, 1579–1661

149

Alone in mountain fastness,
Dozing by the window.
No mere talk uncovers Truth:
The fragrance of those garden plums!

—Bankei, 1622–93

150

One look at plum blossoms
Opened Reiun's eyes,
Old Tan recites poems,
Is often in his cups.
Want "meaningless" Zen?
Just look—at anything!

     —Old Shoju, 1642–1721

151

Spring come again, after moody
Wintering indoors, I left the hermitage
With begging bowl. The village children
Played in long-awaited sun. I bounced
Ball with them, chanting—
One-two-three-four-five-six-seven.
They bounced while I sang, they sang
While I bounced. So I've wasted,
Joyfully, a whole spring day.

     —Ryokan, 1757–1831

NOTES

1. The lumberjacks represent those, including Chindoba's fellow monks, who do not follow properly the way leading to enlightenment, the goal of Zen, suggested by the vision of the crimson flowers.

2, 3. After twenty years of serious application the poet, on rolling the blind, thought he had gained satori. This poem was rejected by his master as an adequate expression of his experience, however, and Chokei wrote poem No. 3, which more than satisfied his master.

4. "I'm through the Gate," i.e., I've had an awakening, with the result that I feel ashamed that, while held in his arms, I have been seeking my "dear old grandpa," the Dharmakaya (Buddha nature).

5. Seeking the "Original Man," i.e., an awakening. Here Chosha echoes Lao Tzu in the *Tao Teh Ching*:

We look and do not see the Way: its name is Colorless.
We listen and do not hear the Way: its name is Soundless.
We grope and do not grasp the Way: its name is Bodiless.

6. Satori lights up the world, and comes with "avoiding thought" or "no-mind" (*wu-hsin*). The Sixth Patriarch, Hui-neng, insisted that meditation should be "pure seeing," which alone discloses truth. One must not look *at* reality, but *as* reality.

7. Enlightenment is a spiritual cleansing, a return to the purity of the Original Self, of which the jewel is a common Zen symbol. It is said that Ikuzanchu gained satori when, while crossing a bridge, he was thrown by his donkey.

8. Though one must prepare oneself in the hope of an awakening, it will never come to one who "frets" about it: whatever one does, wherever one goes, it occurs when one is "ready," never before.

9. The first two lines, from the *Lotus Sutra,* threw the monk into a "great doubt," which often precedes satori but which disappears at once with its attainment—thus the two concluding lines.

10. Bodhidharma (A.D. 470–543?), Zen's First Patriarch, was an Indian monk who arrived in China in the seventh year of the Futsu Era (520), though the date is disputed, some claiming that he arrived during the Liu Sung Era, 420–479. He was the twenty-eighth Patriarch of Indian "Zen" Buddhism, and introduced a school of the philosophy which, combining with the indigenous Chinese Taoism, became Zen. China had received other schools of Buddhism as early as the second century B.C. The Sorei Range was the mountain route over which

Western culture, including Buddhism, entered China. Etsuzan, on looking up at the sunlight in Zephyr Hall, experienced satori, thus was not bound by history or anything else, as suggested by the last two lines.

11. Rodohin's master asked him, "In what way does a grain of millet contain the universe?" [At which Rodohin identified with pure perception.] As Rodohin had been a Taoist, the utensils associated with the philosophy —harp, gourd and bag—are mentioned.

12. Zuigan awakened on hearing his master's question, i.e., answered it by realizing "what comes" within himself. He was astonished to discover, however, that though transformed by the experience he was as if completely dead to himself.

13. Kokuin asked his master, "What happens if I return from Treasure Mountain empty-handed?" The master's reply: "There's a firebrand before each house." Which opened Kokuin's eyes. Satori comes and passes like a stranger on the road, nothing marvelous in itself perhaps yet overwhelming in its effects on one's life. It is a seeing into one's essential nature, a great clarity illuminating the whole of life. It passes like a stranger because it is conceptually ungraspable, in ordinary terms inexpressible—hence the attempts to suggest it in poetry.

14. Not only must one avoid "fretting" about enlightenment, one must forget all about it, along with simple moral categories. Then, as it did to Rijunkyoku, it will come.

15. The first line is a *kigo* (one whose meaning resists conceptualization, expresses satori experience), the second line is meant to suggest the ardent salvationism (golden lion) of the true Zennist. The last two lines mean that the attainment (reaching the North Star) can come only as a result of living calmly and purely in the here and now (represented here by the South Star).

16. Now that Joju has left "mind" and is "refined," he is able to appreciate the genius of Li Po (701–762) the most nonchalant, irresponsible and Zen (or Taoist) spirited poet of T'ang Dynasty China. When "in doubt" Joju could not possibly have understood so free a spirit; now he can. Joju had satori on hearing his master say, "The Buddha and the Patriarchs are no more of two minds than the fist and its clenched fingers."

17. One is reminded by Ritangen's poem of the famous saying of Ch'ing-yuan:

> Before I had studied Zen I saw mountains as mountains, waters as waters. When I learned something of Zen, the mountains were no longer mountains, waters no longer waters. But now that I understand Zen, I am at peace with myself, seeing mountains once again as mountains, waters as waters.

Ritangen's master puzzled him with the question, "Where does life come from?" He awakened when, pointing to his chest, the master cried, "It's in there! That's all you have to know."

18. In gratitude for his awakening, Ryozan bows to the First Patriarch. As in poem No. 7, the gem (or jewel) represents the purity of the Original Self. Zen monks often "time" their meditation by burning incense sticks in front of them, one stick lasting for around half an hour. Usually two or three sticks are burned in a meditation period.

19. An awakening is often preceded by a descent to the depths, the great doubt referred to above, and "precipice" and "abyss" images abound in Zen poetry. With freedom, Koseisoku finds the world "ordinary" once again.

20. Seigensai had satori when he "solved" the koan "Maitreya preaches this." Once one understands, enlightened, the nature of the world, one need no longer depend on others, including one's master. The humor of the first couple of lines gives a sense of the poet's new-found freedom.

21. Ni-buttsu, a nun, had satori when, on asking a question of her master, she was struck and shoved out the door. The last words spoken by the Buddha were, "And now, O priests, I take my leave of you; all the constituents of being are transitory; work out your [own] salvation with diligence." As the preceding piece, this poem proclaims the importance of self-sufficiency, won with satori. Nothing, the delights of the earth themselves, can interfere with that awareness.

22. Tosu had gained no satori for years, and one day was severely reprimanded by his master. With great re-

solve he undertook the strictest kind of discipline for a full month, awakening at the sound of the night bell. There are numerous instances in the history of Zen of similar experiences, a well-known one the subject of the following anecdote:

> For three years Koshu (1839–1905), the great master Gizan's disciple, was unable to gain satori. At the beginning of a special seven-day period of discipline he thought his chance had come, and he climbed the tower of the temple gate, where he made the following vow: "Either I realize my dream up here, or they'll find my dead body at the foot of the tower." He went without food or sleep, giving himself up to constant zazen, but at last had to admit to himself that he had failed. He moved slowly toward the tower railing and slowly lifted a leg over it, at which instant he had an awakening. Overjoyed, he rushed down the stairs and through the rain to Gizan's room. "Bravo!" cried the master before Koshu had a chance to speak. "You've finally had your day!"

The last line of Tosu's poem, a *kigo*, might be interpreted in this way: as the result of satori the poet destroys his illusions, for which the "mud bull" is a traditional symbol. The "coral" here would represent Buddha-wisdom.

23. Ten-i awakened when the pole on which he was carrying two water buckets snapped. The poet's satori made him the match of the great Vimalakirti, whom even a Bodhisattva like Manjusri could not outwit when it came to understanding of "non-duality."

24. Seiken, a government official, was strongly devoted to Zen, and gained enlightenment in the manner described in his poem. Zen has had many distinguished laymen whose attainments are justly celebrated, Dr. D. T. Suzuki and the contemporary poet Shinkichi Takahashi among them.

25. Choro was enlightened upon placing his foot on a brick step. The third line suggests that what he awakened to was not so extraordinary after all, his true self: something to laugh over.

26. Joho had satori when he happened to overhear a fellow monk read aloud the following:

> The great master Yakusan was returning to his temple with a bundle of firewood when a monk asked him, "Where have you been?" Yakusan replied, "I've got firewood." The monk pointed to Yakusan's sword and said, "It sounds tap-tap. What in the world is it?" At which the master unsheathed the sword and assumed a warrior's stance.

Satori, as the last two lines signify, removes all obstacles to Truth, which is everywhere.

27. During mondo (rapid questions and answers) with Master Daie in the latter's room, Kyochu had a thorough awakening when the master let out with a Zen cry. The last line: things are complete in themselves, are not "interchangeable."

28. While grappling with the "oak tree" koan (Monk: "What's the meaning of Bodhidharma's coming over

here?" Joshu: "The oak tree in the courtyard." Cf. the thirty-seventh koan in *Mumonkan*), Chokyusei heard a frog croak and immediately grasped the point of the koan. The master Gensha had satori when, on a mountain path, he tripped on a stone, hurting his foot. Gensha expressed his Zen conviction in this utterance: "Bodhidharma didn't come to China, Eka did not succeed to the patriarchate."

29. As the master Muyo spoke of the koan Joshu's *Mu* (Nothingness), Myotan parted his lips as if to say something, receiving a heavy blow from the master's *shippei* (bamboo stick around three feet long carried by masters for "demonstration purposes") and, then and there, achieving enlightenment. Poisoned drum: the legend is that it kills all who hear it; it symbolizes those utterances of the masters serving to "exterminate" illusions.

30. Waiting to die in the mountains, the master composed this poem while standing on a bridge spanning the Dokei Gorge. As the first two lines indicate, and as was understood by all, the master's death poem was meant to guide his disciples.

31. The Double Peak, the Yellow Plum and the White Omen are mountains where, respectively, the Sixth Patriarch, the Fifth Patriarch and Shien, Seiko's master, had lived. The Law of the last line is the Dharma, made up of the essential principles of Buddhism.

32. Hotei was thought, by some, to be an incarnation of the Bodhisattva Maitreya, the "Buddha of the Future." Bodhisattvas are enlightened beings who, in spite of be-

ing qualified for nirvanic withdrawal from the world, vow to remain among men, in Samsara, until all are free. Hotei wanted with this poem to make his disciples aware of the omnipresent Maitreya.

33. The poem suggests the great freedom that comes with an awakening. Above "life/death" (Samsara), the poet is now able to work for the benefit of all sentient beings.

34. Nansen died on reciting this poem, after having the following dialogue with a monk:

> Monk: Master, where will you be a hundred years from now?
> Nansen: I'll be an ox at the foot of this mountain.
> Monk: May I follow you?
> Nansen: Yes, but make sure to come with a blade of grass gripped between the teeth.

As Dogen wrote in one of the essays in *Shobogenzo* (The Correct-Law Eye Treasury):

> It is fallacious to think that you simply move from birth to death. Birth from the Buddhist point of view, is a temporary point between the preceding and the succeeding; hence it can be called birthlessness. The same holds for death and deathlessness. In life there is nothing more than life, in death nothing more than death: we are being born and are dying at every moment.

35. While sitting in meditation, and just after having said aloud for the benefit of his disciples, "No suppress-

ing arrival, no following departure," Daibai heard a weasel shriek, the "this" of the poem. It is said that on reciting the poem he breathed his last.

36. An anecdote which is often used as a koan may very well illustrate Kiyo's realization that directions, categories and individuation itself are meaningless:

> One day Hyakujo and his master, Baso, saw a flight of wild geese. Baso asked, "Where are they flying?" Hyakujo: "They have already flown away, Master." At this Baso tweaked his disciple's nose until he cried out in pain. Then Baso said, "You claim they have flown away, but they've been there all along, from the very beginning." At this Hyakujo had satori.

The "gray old man" of the poem is Kiyo himself, who though soon to die, will not "go," as he has not "come."

37. Beirei seems to be asserting the fundamental Zen viewpoint that the only thing worth examining, understanding is oneself in the here and now. Trying to understand the Patriarchs, Scripture, etc. is a waste of time, distracts from the real issues of the life of meditation. The objection to "learning" is that it inevitably leads to presuppositions concerning the nature of the world, a philosophy the creation of others, whereas meditation and the pure perception which must accompany it may lead to insight into the very nature of things, the world not yet "created, conceptualized, made philosophy."

38. Godai Chitsu addresses himself in the third line. No longer intimidated by the examples of others, free to

roam in the Absolute, he is his own man. The South Star, and the North, frequently encountered in Zen literature (cf. poem No. 15), are meant to suggest the untrammeled satori mentality.

39. In thirty years Juro would have gained many "disciplinary merits," else he could not have remained at one temple for so long a time. The self-effacing tone of the first two lines is countered by the confidence of the last two. The question "Why did Bodhidharma come from the West?" is often asked, as a koan. Mokuchin's nonchalance has precedence in the founder of one of the three major sects of Zen, the Rinzai (the other two sects—Soto and Obaku), the Master Rinzai:

> Those who are true seekers of the truth must take nothing as Buddhas, Bodhisattvas or Arhats, nothing as admirable in the world. They are to be completely independent, unconcerned. They should smash the Buddhas, Bodhisattvas and Arhats, attaining freedom only when they have attained freedom from them.

40. The first two lines refer to Buddha's important doctrine, "Origination in a Sequential Series," in which the individual is seen as a combination of name and form, the former including all the subjective phenomena of thought and feeling, the latter standing for the four elements of physical nature (earth, water, fire, air). It is karma which unites the components of an "individual" and preserves its identity. Buddhism's purpose is to destroy karma, dissolve the elements. In the last line the

poet expresses total (and contented) resignation by referring to the crematory fire meant for his body after death.

41. Ryuko, solicitous to the last, maintains for the benefit of his disciples the importance of moderation, the need for self-discipline. His poem is offered as an example of the kind written by perhaps less than exceptional but nonetheless influential Zen masters who, by the example of their lives, assure the perpetuation of the philosophy.

42. The first two lines suggest the poet's philosophical freedom. Whenever it is proper to do so, he can push aside the mat used when he is wearing his Buddhist robe. Though the moment appears to be a highly dramatic one, yet all remains calm, empty. Emptiness or Nothingness in Zen, as space in its art, is both vibrant with motion and motionless, formless and yet the source of all form. When called the Void, as in so much Zen poetry, it is the condition of the Dharmakaya, by which all things are stripped of their individuating qualities to their essential selves.

43. Though a death poem, the first line describes the effects on the meditator of *samadhi,* a state reached when the mind has fully exhausted the phenomenal aspects of object or idea and reaches, figuratively, a dead end. Etsuzan seems to be saying that his life can be described in similar terms: he has reached the Source. Today is simply today, tomorrow simply tomorrow. Or as Unmon said, in the Sixth Koan of the *Hekiganroku,* "Every day is a good day."

44. When the sun was at its height, Gyozan died, thus was conscious of his impermanence. As Buddhaghosa, the fifth-century Indian monk, wrote in *Vissudhi Magga* (Way of Purity):

> The life of a living being is exceedingly brief, lasting only while a thought lasts. Just as a chariot wheel rolls at only one point of the tire, and rests at only one point, the life of a being lasts for the period of only one thought.

Throughout Buddhist literature there is a dwelling on impermanence.

45. The poet, above petty "choosing" between life and death, knows that few would understand his "parting words," for in his realization of the Truth he is with the galaxy itself, or so the symbolism of the last lines would seem to indicate.

46. The "silvery world," the realm of purity, can be taken as subject, the "golden body" as object. "Light" and "dark" in the third line represent the many and the one respectively: once they are effaced there can be neither shining nor non-shining. The "sun" symbolizes Shuzan's serene state of satori at the moment of death. Shuzan announced at midday on December 4 that he would die on exactly the same day a year later, which after reciting this poem he did. In the history of Zen there are a number of such occurrences, and yet they are never less than astonishing.

47. The Jewel(ly) Hare stands for the moon, from the popular legend that there are hares on it. The master's stoic, almost joyous acceptance of his coming death is very much in the spirit of Zen.

48. Mount Sumeru occupies the center of the universe in Buddhist cosmology. With such a "mallet" held in his hand, nothing can stop Shonen. At his death (hiding), he will not—unlike the "snared" sun—be seen again, which from the karmic point of view is to be desired.

49. Issan's great self-confidence is maintained to the very end. "Arrow flashing" is a reference to the moment of his death, when he will have no doubt about the nonexistence of earth and sky (life/death, coming/leaving).

50. The last two lines express Tomei's serenity at the moment of death, "clouds" here suggesting birth/death. The master, like Dogen in the passage above, knows that "we are being born and are dying at every moment." Tomei appears to be ready for the inevitable, and his poem, as all death poems, is intended to place disciples on the right path, whose end, if viewed correctly, need not induce fear.

51. Sogen wrote this poem when, late in the thirteenth century, the soldiers of Gen broke into his temple and threatened to put him to the sword. About to die, enter the Void, he is completely without fear, indeed welcomes the "Sword of Gen." The soldiers, awed by the master's fearlessness, left the temple without touching him.

52. The "ancient tune of Ji Peak" is produced by the poet's Zen mind. Daisen lived on Ji Peak. "Spring Time" etc. are famous old melodies of China. The poet seems to be addressing his poem to one of the Patriarchs. "A, B, C" etc. suggest supreme "soundless" music, which Daisen asks us to hear with Zen-attuned ears.

53, 54. In ancient China the so-called "four recluses," fishermen, farmers, woodcutters and herdsmen, were held in great esteem by Taoists and Zennists. Indeed, the greatest of Zen Patriarchs after Bodhidharma himself, the Sixth, Hui-neng (683–713), was a woodcutter, and as his story, as given in the *Platform Sutra,* amply illustrates, all other things being equal a simple woodcutter (or fisherman), who necessarily discovered the Truth for himself, was to be preferred to the scholar of the Scriptures like Shen-hsiu, over whom Hui-neng was chosen as the Sixth Patriarch.

55. The "grand Dream Palace" is the human body, its "six windows" representing the Buddhist six senses, including mind or intellect. The symbolism is common in Zen poetry, as in the seventeenth-century Japanese master Fugai's piece:

Only the Zen man knows tranquillity:
The world-consuming flame can't reach this valley.
Under a breezy limb, the windows of
The flesh shut firm, I dream, wake, dream.

56. The Transplant(ed) Peak, where Kaiseki lived, was in Buddhist legend very famous as the peak which had flown over to China from Mount Vulture in India, sym-

bolizing the complete transmission (transplanting) of the Dharma. The poem is unusual for its show of "attached" compassion, the degree of humanity it reveals. Which suggests among other things a trainee's pre-satori days, when extreme hardships must be borne.

57. Mid Stream was the name of a temple on the Ko River. Dragon Pool was near Seigan's temple. The poet seems to be cautioning the "monk departing for Mid Stream" not to try to share the "woodcutter's song," which would be beyond them because of its mystical import, with the fishermen, who, in this poem, are unlike those of Nos. 53 and 54, symbolic of enlightened Zen men. Here the woodcutter is the genuine Zennist.

58. In ancient China there were four kinds of priests: musicians, go players, poets and painters. In one or more of these arts the priest was expected to excel. The Chinese lute had thirteen notes. "The Crane's Hatred" was a greatly prized melody for the lute.

59. "Returning to a Hermitage" means a solitary retreat, usually of long duration, after the attainment of enlightenment. The poem suggests strongly the contentment following what to a Zennist is the most important experience possible.

60. The poem is an example of a class of poems dealing with the principle that the finger pointing at the moon (i.e., the Scriptures, here) must never be mistaken for the moon itself (the true spiritual experience). Perhaps Bodhidharma's own poem (it is sometimes described as a summary of the whole of his special message, delivered

on his arrival in China) expresses the viewpoint best
of all:

> Transmission outside doctrine,
> No dependence on words,
> Pointing directly at the mind,
> Thus seeing oneself truly, attaining Buddhahood.

61. The poet defends Yomyo's hundred-volume work
Sukyoroku (Religion Mirror Record) against the often
leveled charges of bulkiness and verboseness. The inter-
esting metaphor concluding the poem suggests that Zotan
feels that Yomyo's work, like wine, will mellow with age.

62. "Shooku" (Woodcutter's Hut) was the name of a
fellow monk whom Zotan clearly admired, perhaps en-
vied, for the success with which he had retired from the
world.

63. The poem is especially appealing for the manner in
which it suggests the attitude of an "average" monk, who
while at his monastery cultivates the desired "no-mind"
but, once away from the monastery, is like everyone else
(in mind). Yet he is most confident that he does no
wrong.

64. Mara is in Buddhism the devil. He is always pictured
tempting the meditator, as at the Buddha's own medita-
tion under the Bo-tree when, furious that the Buddha
would not bend, he caused a whirlwind, a rainstorm, a
shower of rocks, etc., to trouble the Buddha, but of course
to no avail. Ingen's poem reveals the inner strength that
came to him with his Zen attainments.

65. The twelfth-century master Suian had the rather remarkable habit of using his fist, on the slow among his followers, to "reveal the truth." He spared none, and one day struck an old woman who was undergoing discipline with him. She died from the blow, and as punishment Suian's temple was razed by the authorities. There is now a paddy field where the temple once stood.

66. The Sento River formed the boundary between the two countries of Go and Etsu in ancient China. The poem implies that Buddhahood, here symbolized by the blue peaks, can be attained only through great application and vigilance.

67. A celebration of satori. The Book of Songs, compiled by Confucius and recommended for ethical teachings, is one of the great books of the ancient world. In this poem the reference is to its "court song" section, prized for its lyricism.

68. The lute signifies in this poem a human: the fingering, his discipline; the perfect melody, his Buddhahood, something which cannot be heard (achieved) with the "parent-begotten" ears. Satori in musical terms is the sudden awakening to this otherwise inaudible melody. Jakuan was the fifth master in the line of Daie (1089–1163).

69. Flying Snow Rock is a fall on Mount Setcho, one of the great mountains of China. Zetsuzo, the fifth master in the line of Shogen (1139–1209), exhorts one to feel the coolness of satori in the midst of sweltering reality.

70. Hokubo is a mountain in China noted for its many tombs. The raw (uncooked) food season: such food was eaten on the 105th day after the winter solstice in memory of Kaishisui, a hermit of Shin, who was burned to death when Bunko (fifth century B.C.), in hope of capturing him, set fire to the mountain slope on which he lived.

71, 72. Ryuge, a tenth-century disciple of the illustrious master Tozan, took it upon himself to spread his master's type of Soto Zen, stressing the importance of prudence and constant awareness. The poem is noteworthy for its calm self-assurance. As is the piece by the same poet which follows, in which the last two lines indicate the degree of his independence: he does not "know" the houses in the village in the sense that he feels no need for what they represent.

73, 74, 75. One of the "Twenty-four Poems of Living in the Mountains" by Zengetsu, among the most popular Zen poets, whose talent extended to painting and calligraphy. As in the two poems which follow, by Sen of Kyuho, this piece gives some sense of the mystic feeling for mountains in the Buddhist communities of East Asia. One of the greatest Buddhist poets of China, Wang Wei (699–759), retired to the mountains to meditate, write and paint (like Zengetsu he was equally celebrated as a painter), producing poems like the following:

The cold mountain turns dark green,
The autumn stream flows on.
Leaning on my staff beyond the gate,
I hear in rushing wind the dying cicada.

*　　*　　*

Not one trace of man on the immense mountain,
Yet human voices come from everywhere.
Throwing shadows on green moss, the sun
Brings distant places to the forest.

*　　*　　*

White pebbles in the river bed,
Leaves reddening in autumn cold:
Though not a drop of rain on the mountain
Path, clothes get damp in such green air.

Then there are the numerous anecdotes about men who
chose to make the mountains their homes, a well-known
one on the Japanese master Fugai (1779–1847), like
Zengetsu and Wang Wei a fine painter:

One day the monk Bundo, fascinated by Fugai's
famous austerities, called at the master's mountain
cave and asked if he could spend the night. The
master seemed happy enough to put him up, and
next morning prepared a breakfast of rice gruel for
him. But not having an extra bowl he left the cave
and a bit later returned with a skull found near a
tomb. Filling it with gruel, he offered it to Bundo,
who refused to touch it, staring at Fugai as if he
thought him mad. At this the master became furi-
ous and drove the monk from the cave with blows.
"Fool!" he shouted after him, "how can you, with
your worldly notions of filth and purity, think your-
self a Buddhist?"

76. The "old gimlet" refers to the Buddha; the "broken ladle" is a symbol of liberation. As is common in poems of awakening, Kakua's enlightenment is expressed with irreverence. Now he is free to think, feel and say what he wants.

77. Kakua expresses the profound sense of wonderment which comes with an awakening, the discovery of the Original Self. As in the case of the Chinese, Japanese Zen poems are very concise. Each line of this piece, for example, contains a metaphor. Though the Japanese language is not wholly monosyllabic, as is Chinese, it employs many Chinese words (*kanji*), and Japanese Zen poetry, which is based on Chinese models, is like the Chinese in every way. Many have remarked on the special character of the Chinese word, its vigor and compactness. What it lacks in "precision," as the result of its many possible meanings, it gains in associational quality and symbolic weight. In Zen poetry this is also true of Japanese.

78. Many Zen poems deal with the most important principle that to "forget" is, in a sense, to "find," that to "let go" is to grasp all the more firmly. The following piece, by Kanemitsu-Kogun, is a good example:

> My hands released at last, the cliff soars
> Ten thousand meters, the plowshare sparks,
> All's consumed with my body. Born again,
> The lanes run straight, the rice well in the ear.

79. All enlightened Zennists speak of the inexpressibility of what they have seen with the "third" or satori-

opened eye. The first instance of truth properly transmitted was the Buddha's Flower Sermon: when the Buddha held up a flower his disciple Mahakasyapa "understood" at once, and his smile was sufficient to convey the depth of his understanding. Once when asked to discourse in the Hall of Meditation, the Chinese master Yokusan declared: "The sutras are explained by sutra experts. I am an expert in the art of silence. Am I not, after all, a Zen master?"

Kakua's "transformation" is well conveyed by the last two lines.

80. Once one has given up the world (the life of deluded action indicated by the first lines) for the contemplative life, one can gain the truth.

81. A powerful expression of the effect on Sogen of his satori. "Nada" (derived from the Sanskrit "Nata") is the demon in Buddhist mythology. The demon subdued, Nada overcome, the poet is dumfounded. "It" of the last line is the Source as realized by Sogen, which when "touched" lights the world. This signifies the unapproachableness of the Source. Sogen, struggling with the koan on Joshu's Nothingness, was awakened by the sound of a wooden announcement board being struck.

82. Enlightenment is the awareness of the Dharmakaya as omnipresent: not only do worldlings face it, they are filled with it. Which is why if they are to be enlightened, they must discover themselves. "Although all men possess this fundamental nature," said Professor Nukariya, late president of the Soto sect Komazawa University, "their different stages of development do not grant them an

equal latitude to express it in their conduct. One can compare the Buddha-nature to the sun, and the individual mind to the sky. The illuminated mind is a beautiful sky in which everything is bathed in sunlight."

83. Guchu awakened on hearing his master's comments on a dialogue between Master Daie and the monk Kozan. The poisoned drum, explained above, is most appropriate here because Kozan means Drum Mount.

84. The pit (earth hole) stands for "fetters of illusion," from which one is delivered by satori. Another poem about the need to "let go," it is notable for its expression of pure freedom. The third line means that once one has had satori one can forget all those things, including proper attitudes, which prepared one for the experience. Nevertheless one continues to sit in Zen after satori: otherwise the experience may become a mere memory.

85. The seeker after enlightenment is asked by his master to find the face he had before he was born, his "Original Face." The "winging bird" denotes freedom; the third line concerns "suchness" (things as they are) and the fourth questions "Nothingness." Free now, Tokugaku, as Keso in poem 84, examines the worth of all leading to the attainment of freedom. Such an attitude suggests the Buddha's great "Parable of the Raft" (from the Majjhima-nikaya of the *Tripitaka*:

What should that man [one who has been enlightened] do, monks, in order to do what should be done to the raft [which got him to the "other shore"]? In this case, monks, [he] may think:

"Suppose that I, having beached this raft on dry ground, or having immersed it in the water, should proceed on my journey? Or suppose that, the raft having been very useful, I should take it with me, packed on my head and shoulders, on my journey?" Monks, a man doing the former and not the latter would be doing the right thing. You, monks, by understanding the parable of the raft, must discard even right states of mind and, all the more, wrong states of mind.

86. Another expression of the pure freedom, with everything seen as it really is and not as we have been conditioned to see it, that comes with the attainment of satori.

87. This moving poem celebrates, in more traditional terms (the lotus is the symbol of Buddhism), the gaining of the Way. The lotus is naturally important to many Zen poems, as the Japanese master Tokuo's:

> The town's aflame with summer heat,
> But Mount Koma is steeped in snow.
> Such is a Zen man's daily life—
> The lotus survives all earthly fire.

Taiko's satori is conveyed by "the flaming lotus," Tokuo's Zen contentment by a "cool" lotus.

88. "Unmon's barrier" is to be found in the eighth koan of *Hekiganroku*, a Chinese work of great antiquity composed of one hundred Zen stories with commentar-

ies. Daito, who gained satori as the result of solving the koan, wrote more than one poem on the subject. Here is another:

At last I've broken Unmon's barrier!
There's exit everywhere—east, west; north, south.
In at morning, out at evening; neither host nor guest.
My every step stirs up a little breeze.

The text of the koan:

> Attention! Suigan, at the end of the summer, spoke to the assembly and said: For the whole summer I have lectured to the brethren. Look! Has Suigan any eyebrows? Hofuko said: He who does robberies has a heart of deceit. Chokei said: They grow. Unmon said: A barrier!

It was on this koan that Daito was asked to meditate by his master, and his poem(s) on the subject served as interpretations of the koan, to be presented to his master for approval. Such is the source of most satori poems.

89. Giten's poem is based in part on an old Zen dialogue:

> Monk: What's the Right Law eye?
> Master: A broken platter.

The "iron ball" is the sun, hence the second line. A ball is a common Zen symbol, as in Keizan's famous expression of his satori: "A pitch-black ball flies through the night." The third line suggests the transformed eyes of an awakened man.

90. Much has been written about the Zen masters' "cruelty in the service of kindness," blows to the faces of their disciples, etc. This poem expresses perfectly the manner in which the disciple often reacts, sometimes— as a result—attaining satori. It would seem that Toin expressed his joy at the sight of the glittering sky to his master (symbolically behaved as if he had been enlightened), receiving thirty blows of the staff for his pains. The rebuke led to profound meditation and true satori.

91. Keisen's self-mockery is very engaging. The poem surely deals with a very common emotion: the disciple is often angry with his master, but he knows him, nevertheless, as master. Occasionally the disciple may even "best" his master, as the following anecdote illustrates:

> Pointing to the sea, Master Kangan said to his disciple Daichi: "You speak of mind over matter— well, let's see you stop those boats from sailing." Without a word the young disciple pulled the *shoji* [screen] across their view. "Hah," the master smiled, "but you had to use your hands." Still without a word, Daichi then closed his eyes.

92. As elsewhere in this volume the six windows stand for the senses. In rejecting Bassui's satori-like experience, the master Unju "crushed the gem" in his disciple's hand, thus leading him on to a genuine awakening. Further on the subject of satori (from D. T. Suzuki's *Essays in Zen Buddhism*, London, Rider & Co., 1949):

With Zen your whole vision of the world is renewed, but you remain normal as usual. You have merely acquired something new. All your mental faculties work now on a different scheme of which you possess the key. To merit the name of satori the inner revolution must [make the subject] conscious that a true baptism has taken place. The intensity of the sensation is in ratio to the effort [made]. Zen is an affair of character, not intelligence.

When Unju scolded his disciple, he was doing more than putting him in his place—he was preparing him for an awakening. Bassui had satori when, about to give his view on the koan Joshu's Nothingness, he was reprimanded by Unju: "Have you done with your reasoning?"

93. "Body-turning," i.e., escaping a Zen impasse. The body-turning word is one of thirteen such special words or phrases taught in Rinzai Zen. *Kwatz* (*Hay* in Chinese) is a meaningless shout used by Rinzai masters to knock disciples off their perch when it is sensed that the disciples are "mentalizing." The great master Rinzai, who began the practice, spoke of four types of *kwatz*: like a sword cutting the chain of thought; like a crouching lion; like vibrating reeds, or a sounding rod; like a blast, meant to awaken to reality. The master Baso once gave out with so strong a *kwatz* that he deafened his disciple Hyakujo for three days. Masters like Rinzai were also likely to strike disciples with their *shippei* (staff) or bare hands. Rarely were such actions resented (when so, only by the hopeless—from the Zen point of view), and al-

most always they produced the desired effect. *Tan* is a piece of lacquered paper on which the monk places his table service.

94. Iron Mountain is the outermost of the iron-made mountains surrounding Mount Sumeru: Cakravala in Buddhist cosmology, it was something one had to get by in order to reach the center of the world, Mount Sumeru, as in this death poem by Zekkai:

> The void has collapsed upon the earth,
> Stars, burning, shoot across Iron Mountain.
> Turning a somersault, I brush past.

"Karma" in Zen is more symbolic than in the traditional Buddhist or Hindu sense, where it suggests that each instant of existence is directly the result of action performed in a former birth, and in its turn affecting future action, the moral implications being clear to all. The last line, with its vision of Hakutei joined with the Patriarchs, gives a sense of his enlightenment.

95. This joyous poem suggests that Seisen, above being affected by common devices such as the *kwatz* or stick, has gained spiritual peace.

96. Once Daio was able to "forget" the "mechanics" of meditation, he had satori, a vision of the Buddha-nature pervading all. He presented this poem to his master, Kido, who approved of it, proclaiming to Daio's fellow monks—"This monk has a thorough grasp of Zen." Daio went to China at the age of twenty-five in search of a master like the great and austere Kido.

97. The most fully represented master in this collection, Dogen founded the Japanese Soto sect after a stay in China of five years. He is perhaps the most eminent writer on Zen in Japan, as much philosopher as poet. The manner in which he is able to combine the two is well illustrated in his poem based on a sentence from the *Diamond Sutra*, "The mind must operate without abiding anywhere," which Dogen transforms to:

> Coming, going, the waterfowl
> Leaves not a trace,
> Nor does it need a guide.

In this death poem there is the same concreteness, and the poem is as distinguished as everything else in Dogen.

98. Doyu's poem is pure metaphor, giving with remarkable precision a sense of the gravity of his emotion: like the sun which daily comes and goes, the poet has come, will go—after a life of standing "mid-air," contemplative withdrawal.

99. The master, expected by his disciples to utter a last word of wisdom, has too much respect for the mystery of the only thing worth transmitting: "Those who know do not speak," the Taoist credo, is echoed by the last line.

100. Tettsu's life as a Zennist is graphically characterized by the first two lines. Now, facing death, the poet meditates on the world's calm and purity. As in many Zen poems, the moon is symbolic of the Buddha-nature: its light touches all alike.

101. Muju's poem suggests that throughout his long life, as the result of an early awakening, he has been unwaveringly tranquil—realizing that as all men he is but a "bubble on the sea."

102. As has been seen a number of times already, the Void is meditated upon constantly—never more than when facing death—by Zennists. One of the best-known death poems in which it is dealt with is Fumon's:

> Magnificent! Magnificent!
> No one knows the final word.
> The ocean bed's aflame,
> Out of the Void leap wooden lambs.

103. Another example of Zennist irreverence, rejection of authority, this piece is interesting for its mention of Brahma, the god of Hinduism (Brahmanism). Had Isan written, "I piss on Buddha," the point made would have been identical. Zen, as all schools of Buddhism, is a "godless" religion-philosophy. In the *Anguttara-nikaya*, a book of the Pali *Tripitaka*, the Buddha is quoted on the subject of man's dependence on god:

> So, then, owing to the creation of a Supreme Deity men will become murderers, thieves, unchaste, liars, slanderers, abusive, babblers, covetous, malicious, and perverse in views. Thus for those who fall back on the creation of a God as the essential reason, there is neither the desire to do, nor the effort to do, nor necessity to do this deed or abstain from that deed.

104. A poem of this kind can be understood properly only if one knows something of the character of its writer. Ikkyu, the fifteenth-century Rinzai master, was one of the most independent masters in the history of Zen. His life was to say the least irregular and unorthodox, as the following poem shows:

> After ten years in the red-light district,
> How solitary a spell in the mountains.
> I can see clouds a thousand miles away,
> Hear ancient music in the pines.

Such a man was unlikely to suffer fools gladly, and Ikkyu used to rail at those who, having no true understanding of Zen, presided over large monasteries. Even in his last poem he could not refrain from ridiculing Master Kido.

105. Issan's supreme confidence, reaching almost to the point of arrogance, is indicated by this poem. One who has been able to "engulf" Buddhas and Patriarchs may very well disturb the universe itself when he passes into nirvana (the last two lines).

106. Against the "fact" of that wind all talk of living and dying seems meaningless. The contemporary Japanese Zen poet Shinkichi Takahashi writes:

> The wind blows hard among the pines
> Toward the beginning
> Of an endless past.
> Listen: you've heard everything.

107. Throughout Buddhist literature, including Zen, there is a denial that one can learn anything of importance from others, as in the remarkable dialogue between the Buddha and Malunkyaputta in *Questions Which Tend Not to Edification* from the *Majjhima-nikaya*, where the man asking inessential questions is likened to one who, struck by a poisoned arrow, asks not that it be pulled out of him at once but insists on knowing the caste of the man who shot the arrow, etc. After reaching in Zen a state where one unlearns all that has been learned, one leaps into the "Great Affirmation," which is beyond knowledge and ignorance.

108. There is a kind of bitter humor, and much self-mockery, in Koho's poem. Another example of the manner in which a death poem can sum up a life. The second line reminds one of a passage in the seventeenth-century master Manzan's *Letter to Jissan* (Jissan: a monk's name, suggesting "real practice"):

First of all, I ask you to look upon the world's riches as a dunghill, upon the most beautiful men and women as stinking corpses, upon the highest honors and reputation as an echo, upon the most malicious calumny as the cawing of a crow. Regard yourself as a fan in winter, the universe as a straw dog.

109. Giun has a vision of a personal hell, conscious perhaps of having overdone his abuse of the Scriptures, Zen itself. The three Buddhist hells are made up of, respectively, fire, blood, swords. Giun's reviling was of course for the benefit of seekers after truth, hence his willingness to plunge into hell—if that's what is deserved.

110. Gizan's final vision, which should be clear to all (the third line), is of a world permeated by Dharmakaya. "Moon in the water," i.e., non-self-nature, something which cannot be grasped; "blossom in the sky," non-existent, illusion. One must see the world as it really is.

111. Gyokko has found, in himself, the reason for pure existence, the identity of coming/going, body/mind. His vision is of a world unlimited, without gate or door: a total freedom. A metaphor for freedom in Zen is the "Gateless Gate," as in the famous thirteenth-century Chinese work of that name, *Mumonkan*.

112. The donkey often appears in Zen writing, as in "donkey-tying pole," i.e., trifle. Here "blind donkey" suggests unenlightened man. The first two lines give the idea of "birthlessness," as developed in the writing of the seventeenth-century master Bankei-Eitaku, whose satori resulted in the revelation that he had never been born and thus was free, in his "birthless Buddha-mind," from the world of "coming" and "returning." As he once explained:

> The birthless Buddha-mind can cut any and every knot. The Buddhas of the past, present and future, and all successive patriarchs should be thought of as mere names for what has been born. From the viewpoint of birthlessness, they are of little significance. To live in a state of non-birth is to attain Buddhahood.

113. There is a common misconception regarding the "morality" of Zen, the result of a wrong understanding

of its detachment. Though Zen questions the normal distinctions between right and wrong, from a Zen point of view there is of course a right way and a wrong way to conduct one's life, and there is sinning. Keisen knows that there are things in the way of his "release," and that his life has been lived in illusion. The very fact, however, that he knows, and that on such a momentous occasion says so, is a form of redemption, promising the desired release.

114. Keso's vision of the "flaming fount," the source of spiritual truth, thaws the "icy" man his many difficult years have made of him. The eighteenth-century master Hakuin once described himself, through the use of a similar metaphor, as he was before his awakening: "Freezing in an icefield, stretched thousands of miles in all directions, I was alone, transparent, and could not move."

115. Dogen said of time that it is man's experience of it which gives it form and "duration"—it is otherwise non-existent, and the foremost contemporary Zen poet of Japan, Shinkichi Takahashi, writes in "The Position of the Sparrow":

Because the whole is part, there's not a whole,
Anywhere, that is not part.
And all those happenings a billion years ago,
Are happening now, all around us: time.
Indeed this morning the sparrow hopped about
In that nebulous whirlpool
A million light years hence.

And since the morning is void,
Anything can be. Since mornings
A billion years from now are nothingness,
We can behold them.

116. Just as the Zennist is free of the conception of time, so too, as in Kokan's poem, is he free of the harness of directions, space, etc. We turn to Shinkichi Takahashi again, writing in "Deck," for an illustration:

A sailor goes ashore, walking along
With existence in the palm of his hand.
With nothing under him,
His tapering toes extend,
Then—like a meteor—disappear.
The sailor is free to go anywhere,
No deck is bigger than his hand.

117. Kokuo, in the last two lines, is speaking of where he will "dwell" once dead. The answer is provided by the Void itself, which can be pictured as an ox made of mud. In other words, Kokuo will enter the Void.

118. Though Kogetsu's numskull life has been uneventful, at death he will soar, "smite the blue sky" with his body, i.e., enter the Void.

119. Jittei's great sense of freedom, faced with his coming death, from the complexities of life (shoving a cart against a wall) is strongly conveyed by the image of the "cosmos-ocean." To pulverize Mount Sumeru is to destroy Samsara, the world of life and death, time, etc.

120. The poet's nonchalance comes as a result of his awareness of a new detachment, which makes it possible to go off alone, thus perceiving all about him the Dharmakaya, here symbolized by moonlight. Going off alone, even aloofness, has always been recommended in Buddhist communities, especially for young monks, as in the *Rhinoceros Discourse*:

> Men associate with and serve others for the sake of an object; friends who have no object in view are difficult to obtain. Men are not pure. Let one walk alone like a rhinoceros.

And the Buddha, with foreknowledge of what lay in store as the result of a created attachment, named his only son Rahula (Impediment). Non-attachment is necessary if one is to gain enlightenment, but once it is gained one must return to the world, be involved in its workings, for which the awakening has prepared one.

121. To enter horses and donkeys means to descend to the realm of beasts without losing Buddhahood. To the last Jisso is solicitous, as the final lines show.

122. In his "Song of Enlightenment" Hakuin writes: "Form being formless, whether one goes or returns/ One remains in the 'nowhere else.'" The second line of Eun's poem is especially interesting, its apparent meaning being that the poet, death imminent, turns back to the "nowhere else," the Void. As in other Zen poems, the moon is symbolic of the Dharmakaya.

123. Daio's poem indicates that his confidence was very firm: the world held nothing which could stop him in his quest of the truth. On December 29 the poet, aged seventy-two, said to his disciples, "Today I'm here, coming from nowhere. In exactly one year from today I'll go, without having anywhere to go." On December 29, 1308, Daio wrote this poem, then died.

124. As all masters, Tokken feels at one with the world, the fruit of his achievement as Zennist. He is unafraid of death because—and this the poem strongly suggests— it is as natural for the body to break up as it is for the clouds. Yet the moon, holding symbolically all that is precious, remains to work its wonders on the world, making its various parts one—as in the twentieth-century master Tesshu's poem, written when he visited Sokei, the place in China where the Sixth Patriarch lived:

> The holy earth is overspread with leaves,
> Wind crosses a thousand miles of autumn fields.
> The moon that brushes Mount Sokei silvers,
> This very instant, far Japan.

125. Keizan's poem is metaphorically elaborate: the field represents the mind, which the poet works, i.e., trains, disciplines, the result being that it continues to yield for him. The last line is a vision of himself, in the place of meditation, a "farmer" in his application to the very end.

126. A poem on zazen. The seven Buddhas: Vipassi, Sikhi, Vessabdhu, Kakusandha, Konagamana, Kassapa and Gautama, the present Buddha. Later books such as the *Buddhavamsa* and the introduction to the *Jataka*

Book describe as many as twenty-five Buddhas (Gautama's career as a Bodhisattva began in the time of Dipankara, first of these, when Gautama was a hermit called Sumedha). What characterizes Dogen's Soto Zen is "simply sitting," so called, in contrast to the koan examination of Rinzai Zen. The meditator sits cross-legged on a cushion, a master sometimes uses an armrest. The poem served to instruct Dogen's numerous disciples in the proper position of meditation. Many other masters gave such instructions, those of the fourteenth-century master Meiho among the best known:

> In zazen [the student's] legs are crossed so that his Buddha-nature will not be led off by evil thoughts, his hands are linked so that they will not take up sutras or implements, his mouth shut so that he refrain from preaching a word of Dharma or uttering blasphemies, his eyes half shut so that he not distinguish between objects, his ears closed to the world so that he not hear talk of vice and virtue, his nose as if dead so he not smell good or evil. Since his body has nothing on which to lean, he is indifferent to likes and dislikes. He negates neither being nor non-being. He sits like Buddha on the pedestal, and though distorted ideas may arise from him, they do so idly and are ephemeral, constituting no sin, like reflections in a mirror, leaving no trace.

127. The "Correct-Law Eye Treasury" is another name for the Buddha's Law: the Buddha proclaimed on Mount Vulture, "I have the Correct-Law Eye Treasury, the miraculous mind of Nirvana. . . . All this I give to Maha-Kashapa." As in poem 101, by Muju, there is the suggestion of great tranquillity. Dogen was born some

twenty-six years before Muju, and died long before the latter achieved maturity, so there is a possibility that Muju appropriated the great master's metaphor for his poem.

128. While Dogen is revered as *Koso* (high Patriarch) of Soto Zen, Keizan is honored as its *Taiso* (great Patriarch): he founded Soji Temple and wrote often on the nature of mind, as if paraphrasing Dogen's poem in passages such as the following:

> Having no form and in spite of hearing, seeing, knowing, perceiving, the mind is above coming, going, moving, remaining. When you see it in this way, you are beginning to understand the nature of mind. When all discrimination is abandoned, when contact with things is broken, the mind is brighter than sun and moon together, cleaner than frost and snow.

129. Further, on the subject of zazen, we turn again to Meiho:

> Of all good works, zazen comes first, for the merit of only one step into it surpasses that of erecting a thousand temples. Even a moment of sitting will enable you to free yourself from life and death, and your Buddha-nature will appear of itself. Then all you do, perceive, think becomes part of the miraculous Suchness of the world.

130. There is an old Japanese saying, *Shizen ichimi* (Poetry and Zen are one). One can also speak of *Kadō*, or the Way (to the truth) of poetry. Dogen is as great

a poet as he is philosopher, as an image for impermanence such as this poem gives amply shows. Many distinguished Western artists have been awed by the Zennist's power to speak philosophy through poetry and art, Van Gogh among them (in a letter to his brother Theo):

> . . . you see a man who is undoubtedly wise, philosophic, and intelligent, who spends his time how? In studying the distance between the earth and the moon? No. He studies a single blade of grass, [which] leads him to draw every plant and then the seasons, the wide aspects of the countryside, the animals, then the human figure. So he passes his life, and life is too short to do the whole. And you cannot study Japanese art . . . without becoming gayer and happier, and we must return to nature in spite of our education and our work in the world of convention.

131. The poem is based on the forty-sixth case of *Hekiganroku*: Kyosei, a ninth-century Chinese master, on hearing raindrops, asked one of his disciples, "What's that sound?" "Why, raindrops," answered the disciple, showing that while he was not at one with the sound, the master was, the eavesdrops had "entered him." Kyosei, in other words, had attained—in relation to the eavesdrops—the state of *muga*, a total identification which results in a breakdown of all distinctions between subject and object, and a most important step toward satori.

132. "I touch my nose" suggests that Ejo had finally discovered the Original Body, "the face he had before being born." Such a discovery naturally results in a kind

of revulsion: there is now all the more reason to make of oneself something other than a "festering lump." Yet the revulsion, which accompanies the "great doubt" associated with the period before enlightenment, disappears with its attainment. The poet's reference to walking Chinese fashion would seem to mean that he is aware of his past affected ways, which with the acquirement of the straw sandals, and the new outlook symbolically suggested, have ended.

133. Tettsu has made the greatest discovery open to the Zennist, the simple fact that the Buddha does not exist outside one's self. For years he had been "yoked" not only by karmic causality but by the disciplines of the monastery, and had not once glimpsed the Buddha. Now, at last, he has found him—in himself. Though this poem is not designated as an enlightenment poem, it might be read as such. This it shares with many Zen poems.

134. An old Zen poem prized for its suggestiveness. It is a representation of the Original Face, the "unborn." For a man of satori the oriole sings even when silent to normal ears, the plum tree, though dry (seemingly dead), blooms as always. One is reminded of Ikkyu's famous poem based on the phrase "Form in Void" in *The Heart Sutra*:

> The tree is stripped,
> All color, fragrance gone,
> Yet already on the bough,
> Uncaring spring!

And of another well-known waka:

In the depth of night,
The crow's hushed cawing:
My father, my mother.

135. In the original Japanese "good" and "bad" also
mean, respectively, "reed" and "rush." One of the great-
est masters in the history of Japanese Rinzai Zen,
Hakuin was an accomplished painter and poet, as well
as the creator of one of the most original koans for stu-
dents of the philosophy, "What is the sound of one hand
clapping?" The poem says that unless one forgets all such
discriminations as "good" and "bad" one cannot hope to
live contentedly, "taste the evening cool." The poem is
an example of the senryu, like the haiku a seventeen-
syllable piece, but unlike it in prizing wit and humor,
even sarcasm.

136. Shariputra stood foremost in *prajna* (wisdom)
among the Buddha's disciples. "Another ferry" might be
taken as a port like Nagasaki, but as another example
of *kigo* the whole of the poem's final sentence is most
difficult to paraphrase. Hakuin was among the most ver-
satile of the great masters, even producing along with his
disciple Torei a commentary on The Heart Sutra en-
titled A Poisonous Commentary on The Heart Sutra
(Japanese: *Dokugo-chu-shingyo*), "poisonous" because in
his judgment the words of the Buddhas and Patri-
archs were potent enough to "exterminate" both delusion
and enlightenment. Such was his style, whether as com-
mentator or poet.

137. The three poisons: covetousness, anger, ignorance.
The poem was written after Ungo left (perhaps, con-

sidering his state of mind, escaped from) the temple where he had been presiding. The first line would seem to imply that as an active master, forced to deal with disciples and their problems, Ungo was unable to avoid the three poisons, if only as a result of having to prescribe antidotes for them day in, day out. The last lines strongly convey his rediscovered sense of freedom.

138. The theme is non-attachment. Taigan Takayama, in an interview conducted by Takashi Ikemoto and me for the Anchor volume *Zen*, gave some idea of the great importance of that condition:

> Satori will make it possible for you to live constantly in a state of joy. But remember that one needs further discipline to rid oneself of this joy, for there must not be even the shadow of attachment, any kind of attachment, in Zen. In this way you can attain a genuine awakening.

One must not, in other words, be "lured" by anything.

139. The master recited this poem on New Year's Day of the year in which he died. The spring breeze, symbolic in Zen literature as elsewhere of rejuvenation, appears in a remarkable poem by Daigu, the seventeenth-century master:

> Who dares approach the lion's
> Mountain cave? Cold, robust,
> A Zen man through and through,
> I let the spring breeze enter at the gate.

140. Getsuo in this piece sees and hears like a Zennist, yet the poem does not appear to express any profound Zen truth. It must not be assumed, in spite of their seriousness and the gravity of most of their writing, that every time the masters sat down to compose poetry their intention was to probe, or edify disciples.

141. Lake Biwa, near Kyoto, is a very large and superbly situated body of water which is often referred to in Japanese literature. A *ri* is a considerable distance. Reed boat and the Futsu Era: Bodhidharma, in one of the many legends about him, is said to have sailed to China on a reed (small boat) in the Futsu Era, a subject of many paintings as well as poems. The monk of the next to the last line is, of course, Geppa himself, who is completely at one with the landscape.

142. Eno (Japanese for Hui-neng, the Sixth Patriarch) came from Reinan, thus "the Way of Reinan" means Eno's way of achieving enlightenment, the sudden (Southern School) method of discipline and training, to which austerities such as meditating in the wind and snow have always been considered important. Here is how Tenzan Yasuda, a master of Yamaguchi (in an interview made for the Anchor volume *Zen*), describes, in part, his satori:

> It happened on the fifth day of the special December training at Yogenji, while I was engaged in what is called night-sitting. As is sometimes done, a few of us left the meditation hall and, choosing a spot in the deep snow near the river, began our Zen sitting, each of us engrossed in his koan. I was

not conscious of time, nor did I feel the cold. Suddenly the temple bell struck the second hour, time of the first morning service, which we were expected to attend. I tried to get up, but my feet were so numb with cold that I fell to the snow. At that very instant it happened, my satori.

The last lines of Eun's poem give a sense of his awakening.

143. To a disciple's question—a very common one, much like a koan—"What is the Buddha?" Tozan, a Chinese master, replied: "He has a head three feet long and a neck of two inches." In other words the Buddha is formless, above our measuring or imagining. Tozan might have answered, in the spirit in which the question has almost always been answered in mondos (questions and answers, in dialogues between masters and disciples, with a premium placed on swiftness and inventiveness), "A brick." Here is one of the best-known examples of mondo:

One day Baso, a disciple of Ejo, the Chinese master, was asked by the master why he spent so much time meditating.
Baso: "To become a Buddha."
The master picked up a brick and began rubbing it very hard. It was now Baso's turn to ask a question: "Why," he asked, "do you rub that brick?"
"To make a mirror."
"But surely," protested Baso, "no amount of polishing will make a brick into a mirror."
"Just so," said the master: "no amount of sitting cross-legged will make *you* into a Buddha."

144. Bunan, in this poem, writes as simply and directly, on the subject of non-attachment, as he writes in the following much-prized pieces on *muga* and the extinction of "self" which accompanies it, indeed makes such identification possible:

> The moon's the same old moon,
> The flowers exactly as they were,
> Yet I've become the thingness
> Of all the things I see!

*　*　*

> When you're both alive and dead,
> Thoroughly dead to yourself,
> How superb
> The smallest pleasure!

145. In this poem Bunan speaks, presumably for the benefit of a layman, of the paradox that the mind is easily chained to that which is designed to free it, something all Zennists must learn to cope with and, eventually, overcome.

146. It would appear that the poet is expressing an elitist view. The Sixth Patriarch himself said (in the *Platform Sutra*):

> There is no distinction between sudden enlightenment [his own method] and gradual enlightenment [the Northern School method, a rival one] in the Law, except that some people are intelligent and others stupid. Those who are ignorant realize the truth gradually, while the enlightened ones attain it suddenly.

147. The poet compares himself, as enlightened master, with the two famous Chinese masters Mugo and Zuigan. The former always gave his followers the same advice, the latter trained himself by having daily the following dialogue with himself (*Mumonkan*, Koan twelve): "My master!" "Yes, sir!" "Be wide awake!" "Yes, sir!" "And from now on don't let anyone deceive you!" "Yes, sir! Yes, sir!" The poem suggests the varying needs of Zen men, as men seeking the truth, as well as their distinct personalities.

148. For a very long time Gudo, despite his best efforts, was unable to gain satori, more than once wanting to end his life. He awakened at the age of twenty-nine, nonetheless, and henceforth led a life of "mindlessness." The last line reminds one of the last line of Hakuin's poem:

> Priceless is one's incantation,
> Turning a red-hot iron ball to butter oil.
> Heaven? Purgatory? Hell?
> Snowflakes fallen on the hearth fire.

Both were probably suggested by the expression, symbolic of impermanence, "A snowflake fallen on the hearth fire" (*Hekiganroku*, Koan sixty-nine).

149. Dr. Suzuki wrote of Bankei: "In the whole history of Zen, in China and Japan, there is none, it might be said, who has displayed so independent a view." He is sometimes spoken of as, along with Dogen and Hakuin, one of the three great Zen masters of Japan: if Dogen is a profound dialectician, and Hakuin a robust poet and

painter, then Bankei might be called an intuitionist, pure and simple, whose Zen of "Birthlessness" has always had a profound appeal to simple and sophisticated alike. It is said that Bankei had consummate satori on smelling the scent of plum blossom, thus the significance of the last line. As an example of his independent view (quoted from his *Sayings and Writings,* compiled and edited by Dr. Suzuki as one of the volumes of the Iwanami Library, only part of which has appeared in English translation):

> One's everyday life, in its entirety, should be thought of as a kind of sitting in Zen. Even during formal sitting, one may leave one's seat to attend to something. In my temple, at least, such things are allowed. Indeed it's sometimes advisable to walk in Zen for one incense stick's burning, and sit in Zen for the other. A natural thing, after all. One can't sleep all day, so one rises. One can't talk all day, so one engages in zazen. There are no binding rules here.

150. If for no other reason, Shoju-rojin (Old Shoju) would be known as one of the most eminent Zen masters of Japan because it was under him that Hakuin brought his Zen understanding to full maturity. He was known as a rigorous disciplinarian, which was why the troubled Hakuin sought him out as a spiritual mentor. Reiun is a typical old Zen master of China. "Tan" comes from Dokyo Etan, which was Shoju's full Buddhist name; thus "Old Tan" is another name for the poet. "Meaningless" Zen is the only true Zen, the moon and not the pointing finger.

151. Ryokan, a beloved hermit monk, is famous for his freedom and nonchalance. Here is another of his poems:

Without a jot of ambition left
I let my nature flow where it will.
There are ten days of rice in my bag
And, by the hearth, a bundle of firewood.
Who prattles of illusion or nirvana?
Forgetting the equal dusts of name and fortune,
Listening to the night rain on the roof of my hut,
I sit at ease, both legs stretched out.

O15